Mozart

The Life and Music of the Great Composer

(The Lives and Legacies of History's Most Famous Composers)

Steven Williams

Published By **Phil Dawson**

Steven Williams

All Rights Reserved

Mozart: The Life and Music of the Great Composer (The Lives and Legacies of History's Most Famous Composers)

ISBN 978-1-77485-785-4

No part of this guidebook shall be reproduced in any form without permission in writing from the publisher except in the case of brief quotations embodied in critical articles or reviews.

Legal & Disclaimer

The information contained in this ebook is not designed to replace or take the place of any form of medicine or professional medical advice. The information in this ebook has been provided for educational & entertainment purposes only.

The information contained in this book has been compiled from sources deemed reliable, and it is accurate to the best of the Author's knowledge; however, the Author cannot guarantee its accuracy and validity and cannot be held liable for any errors or omissions. Changes are periodically made to this book. You must consult your doctor or get professional medical advice before using any of the suggested remedies, techniques, or information in this book.

Upon using the information contained in this book, you agree to hold harmless the Author from and against any damages, costs, and expenses, including any legal fees potentially resulting from the application of any of the information provided by this guide. This disclaimer applies to any damages or injury caused by the use and application, whether directly or indirectly, of any advice or information presented, whether for breach of contract, tort, negligence, personal injury, criminal intent, or under any other cause of action.

You agree to accept all risks of using the information presented inside this book. You need to consult a professional medical practitioner in order to ensure you are both able and healthy enough to participate in this program.

TABLE OF CONTENTS

Introduction 1

Chapter 1: Who Was Mozart? 2

Chapter 2: Youngster And Early Music Career 5

Chapter 3: His Time In Vienna 16

Chapter 4: Final Years As A Music Industry 27

Chapter 5: His Personality And His Character 34

Chapter 6: The Style And The Simple Ness Of His Character 38

Chapter 7: The Grand Tour 1763-66 60

Chapter 8: More Journeys To Italy 103

Chapter 9: Mature Style 1786-90 154

Conclusion 184

Introduction

Wolfgang Amadeus Mozart was probably the most gifted musician that has ever lived, with the musical ability that can only be imagined.

He was not just a brilliant composer as well as a superb pianist who wowed the audience of his time by his talents.

Contrary to other composers, Mozart was not interested in creating new forms of music. He determined to compose as close to perfect as feasible. Many would say Mozart achieved perfectionism.

In spite of his amazing talents, Mozart was just a human being just like everyone else. He was arrogant and rude and was not an incredibly attractive person. However, he composed music that was unlike any music that was heard before , and is still loved today nearly 200 years after the time he passed away.

I hope that the information below will enthral you and inspire you to learn further regarding Mozart and his amazing music.

Chapter 1: Who Was Mozart?

Perhaps you've heard Mozart's music or you've heard about his work in your history class. Nearly everyone across the globe knows at a minimum about Mozart. Therefore, let's talk about our knowledge of Mozart and give an overview of his life, his work and his legacy.

Wolfgang Amadeus Mozart (27 January 1756-5 December 1791) was baptized Johannes Chrysostomus Wolfgangus theophilus Mozart was a revered and well-known composer from the Classical period.

Born in Salzburg in Salzburg, in the Holy Roman Empire, Mozart showed extraordinary talent at an early age. He was already proficient on the keyboard and the violin, he picked at the age of five and appeared before European royalty. He then embarked on an extravagant excursion. At the age of 17, Mozart was appointed a an artist in the Salzburg court, but began to feel nervous and decided to go seeking a more prestigious place.

When he was examining Vienna the year 1781, his employer removed from his Salzburg post in 1781. He decided to stay in Vienna and gained some fame but had no financial security. In his final period in Vienna, he composed many of his most well-known concertos, symphonies, operas, and even portions of the Requiem that were mostly unfinished when he passed away. sudden death at 35. The circumstances of his death have been largely uncertain and are the reason why they have been extensively distorted.

Despite the sudden passing of his body and his speedy construction led to over 600 pieces that were in the genre that he composed at the time. Many of these are regarded as the top of the concertante, symphonic operatic, chamber and choral collections. He is regarded as one of the greatest classical composers in perpetuity and his influence in Western music is significant particularly with regard to Ludwig van Beethoven. His former coworker Joseph Haydn wrote: "posterity will not see this skill ever again until one hundred years from now".

Chapter 2: Youngster And Early Music Career

Wolfgang Amadeus Mozart was born on the 27th of January 1756. He was the son of Leopold Mozart (1719-- 1787) and Anna Maria, nee Pertl (17201720- 1778) in Getreidegasse 9 in Salzburg. Salzburg is the city that was capital city of the Archbishopric Salzburg and was an ecclesiastical Principality within the Holy Roman Empire (today in Austria). He was the eldest of seven children, five of whom perished when they were infants. His older sibling was Maria Anna Mozart (1751-1829) who was known as "Nannerl". Mozart was baptized the day following his birth at St. Rupert's Cathedral in Salzburg. The baptismal record reveals his name as a Latinized form, namely Joannes Chrysostomus Wolfgangus Theophilus Mozart. He was known as "Wolfgang Mozart" when he was an adult, however, his name was a variety of variations.

Leopold Mozart, a local of Augsburg which was then as an Imperial Free City in the Holy Roman Empire, was a modest composer and expert teacher. The year 1743 was the time he received a call as the 4th violinist of the musical facilities of the Count Leopold Anton von Firmian, the highest prince-archbishop of Salzburg. After four years was his wedding to Anna Maria in Salzburg. Leopold was appointed his orchestra's assistant Kapellmeister in 1763. The year in which his son was born, Leopold released a violin book called Versuch einer grundlichen Violinschule, that was a huge success.

When Nannerl was seven, she began piano classes with her father while her brother, who was three, searched. A few years later, following her brother's passing she reflected on the time:

He would often be on the clavier, picking thirds that was always a challenge and his joy was apparent that it sounded great. ...

In the fourth year of his life, his father, in the course of the sake of a game began to teach him a few tricks and pieces of the clavier. ... He was able to play it easily and with the finest unique, and he was able to keep on time. ... When he was 5 years old He was already creating small pieces of music, which was played to his father who recorded them.

The first compositions, K. 1-5 - 5, were recorded within the Notenbuch of Nannerl. There is some debate in the academic community regarding the question of whether Mozart was between 4 and 5 years old when he composed his first musical structures but there's no evidence to suggest the fact that Mozart composed his first three works of music in a few weeks after each other.

In his early days Wolfgang's father was his sole instructor. Alongside music and teaching his children subjects in scholastics and languages. Solomon says that while Leopold was a committed teacher to his children, there is evidence that Mozart was always eager to go beyond what he was taught. The first structure he ink-spattered as well as his quick-witted efforts on the violin were the result of his own efforts and came as surprising to Leopold who eventually gave up any compensation after his son's talents became apparent.

1762-73 Travel
The main short article is: Mozart family grand trip and Mozart in Italy
When Wolfgang was still a young man and his family travelled on European travels where Wolfgang and Nannerl played as prodigies for kids. The first was an exhibition in 1762 in the Prince-elector's court Maximilian III of Bavaria in Munich and also during the Imperial Courts in Vienna and Prague. A lengthy show tour followed with a duration of three years and six months following that which took their family members to court in Munich, Mannheim, Paris, London, Dover, The Hague, Amsterdam, Utrecht, Mechelen

and again to Paris returning to home via Zurich, Donaueschingen, and Munich. In the course of this journey, Wolfgang met a lot of musicians and acquainted himself with works by other composers. The most significant influence came from Johann Christian Bach, whom visited in London between 1764 and in 1765. When he was just 8 years old old, Mozart wrote his first Symphony, the bulk of which was probably transcribing by his father.

The journeys of the family were generally difficult, and the travel conditions were basic. They were required to wait for invitations and payment from the nobility and suffered long illness that was near fatal away from home. First Leopold (London in the summer of 1764, during the summer months) and then the two kids (The Hague, in the fall of 1765). The family returned to Vienna in 1767, and was there until the end of December 1768.

After a calendar year living within Salzburg, Leopold and Wolfgang embarked on a journey to Italy after which they left Anna Maria and Nannerl in the family home. The trip ran from December 1769 through March 1771. Similar to previous trips, Leopold wanted to show his son's talents as an entertainer and rapidly growing composer. Wolfgang was introduced to Josef Myslivecek and Giovanni Battista Martini in Bologna and was accepted as a part of the renowned Accademia Filarmonica. In Rome the composer listened to the music of Gregorio Allegri's Miserere twice, with great efficiency at the Sistine Chapel, and wrote the score from memory, thereby creating the first copy that was not approved by this treasured possession belonging to the Vatican.

The year 1770 was the time in Milan, Mozart wrote the opera Mitridate,'re di Ponto (1770) that was staged with great success. This led to more opera-related orders. The father and son traveled twice to Milan (Augustto the month of December in 1771 and from October

March 1773) to study the bests and structure from Ascanio from Alba (1771) as well as Lucio Silla (1772). Leopold believed that these trips could lead to an appointment by a professional for his child. probably the archduke ruling Ferdinand was contemplating hiring Mozart however, due to his mother Empress Maria Theresa's insistence that she would not make use of "pointless people" the issue was thrown out and Leopold's dreams weren't fulfilled. At the conclusion of the trip, Mozart wrote the solo motet Exsultate Jubilate, Exsultate, K. 165.

1773- 77 The work in the Salzburg court

After reuniting with his father from Italy on the 13th March 1773 Mozart became an artist for the court of the governor of Salzburg the Prince Archbishop Hieronymus Colloredo. Mozart was surrounded by many wonderful admirers and acquaintances in Salzburg and was able to write in various categories, including sonatas, symphonies and symphonies as quartets, mass serenades, as well as a variety of small operas. Between November 1775 and December 1775, Mozart discovered a love for violin concertos. He wrote five concertos (the only one he wrote) that gradually increased in musical sophistication. The final three3 - K. K. 216, K. 218 and K. 219have become staples in the collection. He began his career in 1776 and began his attention towards piano concertos, which culminated at K. 271 which was the E Concerto K. 271 in 1777 that was considered by critics as an experiment in composition.

Despite these achievements, Mozart grew significantly dissatisfied with Salzburg and intensified his efforts to secure another job. One reason for this was his modest earnings of just 150 florins per year. Mozart was aspired to write operas and Salzburg offered only a few occasions to perform such. The situation grew more dire in 1775 , when the court theatre closed in particular because the second theatre situated in Salzburg was mostly used for the purpose of observing performers.

Two lengthy explorations in search of work interrupted the long Salzburg stay. Mozart and his father travelled to Vienna from 14 July to 26 September 1773 as well as Munich from December 6 until March 1775. The check-outs did not have great success, but the Munich trip resulted in an iconic success by Mozart's best operetta La finta giardiniera.

1777-78: Travel to Paris

In August 1777 Mozart quit his job at Salzburg and, on September 23, returned to the city to find work. He made excursions to Augsburg, Mannheim, Paris and Munich.

Mozart was eventually able to be acquainted by the members of the renowned orchestra from Mannheim one of the most prestigious of its kind in Europe that time. He also fell in love with AloysiaWeber, one of the four daughters of the musical family. There were potential clients of his the work of Mannheim however, they didn't come to anything which is why Mozart went to Paris on the 14th of March, 1778 to pursue his quest. The letters he received from Paris suggest a possible job as organist at Versailles However, Mozart was not enthralled by the prospect of a meeting with Versailles. He was immediately in financial debt and was forced to loan his belongings. The lowest point of the go to was when Mozart's mother was taken down with illness and passed away in 1778 on the 3rd of July. There were delays regarding contacting a doctorwhich, most likely according to Halliwell due to an inability to pay. Mozart was adamant about Melchior Grimm, who in his capacity as the individual secretary to the Duke d'Orleans was a resident of his estate.

When Mozart is in Paris and his father was looking for his employment in Salzburg. With the assistance of the nobility of the region, Mozart was offered a job as organist in the court and concertmaster. The annual salary was 450 florins, however Mozart was hesitant to accept. In the meantime, the relationship among Grimm and Mozart were cooling, and Mozart had left. After departing Paris in 1778 to go to Strasbourg and then Mannheim, Mozart remained at Mannheim and Munich and still wanted to have a meeting outside of Salzburg. In Munich the following year, he met Aloysia who was now an powerful singer however, she wasn't as enthralled by Mozart. Mozart eventually returned to Salzburg on January 15 in 1779, and he used his new position, however his displeasure with Salzburg was not diminished.

Chapter 3: His Time In Vienna

In Jan. 1781 Mozart's work Idomeneo was premiered to "significant popularity" during the city of Munich. In March 1781, Mozart was summoned to Vienna in the presence of his patron was Archbishop Colloredo was a part of the ceremonies in preparation for the accession ceremony of Joseph II to the Austrian throne. For Colloredo it was simply the case of wanting his musical assistant to be present (Mozart certainly had to dine at the Colloredo's establishment alongside the cooks and valets). However, Mozart was planning a more lucrative career, even though his archbishop's office. For instance Mozart wrote to his father:

My first goal now is to greet the emperor in a professional manner and I'm certain that he will be comfortable with me. I'd be so thrilled to play my opera to him and afterwards perform a fugue or two as that's the kind of music he enjoys.

Mozart certainly did encounter the Emperor and was able to help his profession substantially through commissions as well as a part-time post.

In the exact same letter to his dad just quoted, Mozart detailed his strategies to get involved as a musician in the shows of the Tonkunstler-Societat, a popular advantage show series; this plan too occurred after the regional nobility dominated on Colloredo to drop his opposition.

Colloredo's need to stop Mozart in performing at a location outside of his facility was, in other instances however, he was able to carry it out and caused the composer to be angry and causing him to lose an opportunity to perform in front of the Emperor at the Countess Thun's for a fee equal to the half that of the Salzburg salary.

The dispute with the archbishop was resolved in May. Mozart attempted to quit, but was rejected. In the following month, his consent was granted however in an extremely offensive manner Mozart was exiled "with an assault on the arse" and executed by the archbishop's deputy and The Count Arco. Mozart was able to settle in Vienna as a performer on a contract basis and composer.

The dispute with Colloredo was more difficult for Mozart because his father sided against his. He was adamant to be a follower of Colloredo and return to Salzburg Mozart's father exchanged extremist letters with his son and he was locked up by their company. Mozart was adamantly defending his decision to pursue an independent career in Vienna. The conflict was resolved with Mozart had his resignation dismissed by an archbishop and released him from both his business as well as his father's need to return. Solomon describes Mozart's resignation as an "advanced step" that significantly altered his life.

More information about the early years
Mozart's new job in Vienna was a success from the beginning. He usually performed as piano player, particularly during a game before the Emperor Muzio Clementi on December 24, 1781. He quickly "had become the top pianist within Vienna". Mozart also achieved success as a composer and in 1782 he completed the opera Die Entfuhrung from the Serail (" The Kidnapping from the Seraglio") that was premiered on the 16th of July in 1782, and enjoyed a hefty amount of success. The opera was soon presented "throughout the German-speaking Europe" and totally made Mozart's name a household composer.

At the peak of his squabbles in Colloredo, Mozart relocated to the Weber family who had moved into Vienna following his departure from Mannheim. The father of the family, Fridolin, had passed to death as did the Webers were welcoming guests to pay for their expenses.

His Wedding and His Kids

Not being able to get married to AloysiaWeber, who was married to the famous artist and star Joseph Lange, Mozart's interest transferred to the 3rd girl in the family Constanze.

The courtship did not go well; but the fact that it took place via correspondence, it is possible the possibility that Mozart and Constanze were briefly separated during the month of April in 1782. Mozart had a difficult task of gaining his dad's approval to marry. The couple was finally married on the 4th of August, 1782 at St. Stephen's Cathedral, the day prior to when his father's consenting letter arrived through the post. [55]

The couple was blessed with 6 children from which only 2 were born:

Raimund Leopold (17 Juneto 19th August, 1783).

Karl Thomas Mozart (21 September 1784-- 31 October 1858).

Johann Thomas Leopold (18 Octoberto 15 November, 1786).

Theresia Constanzia Adelheid Friedericke Anna (27 December 1787- 29 June 1788).

Anna Maria (passed away not long after her birth, 16 Nov 1789).

Franz Xaver Wolfgang Mozart (26 July 1791- 29 July 1844).

1782-- 87.

Between 1782 and 1783 Mozart became acquainted with the works from Johann Sebastian Bach and George Frideric Handel because of the influence on Gottfried van Swieten who had many of the documents of those Baroque masters. Mozart's study of these scores had an impact on the structures that were written in the Baroque style, and then influenced his musical vocabulary such as in passages that are fugal in Die Zauberflote (" The Magic Flute") and the conclusion in Symphony No. 41.

It was 1783 when Mozart along with his wife visited their family members in Salzburg. The family of his father and sister was very kind to Constanze however, the fact that they checked out set off the development for one Mozart's greatest liturgical works, the Mass in C minor. Although it was the work was not yet completed the piece was performed in Salzburg and Constanze sang an individual part.

Mozart was a frequent visitor to Joseph Haydn in Vienna around 1784. The two composers remained close friends. As Haydn visited Vienna and Mozart visited, they often were in a informal string quartet that was not written. Mozart's 6 quartets dedicated to Haydn originate from 1782-1785, and are believed as a reaction in Haydn's Opus 33 set from 1781. Haydn in 1785 wrote Mozart's father: "I tell you before God that, as a true man, your son is the greatest composer I have ever heard of to me through the individuality and importance as he has taste and the highest capability in composition."

From 1782 to 1785 Mozart performed shows with himself as a musician. He performed three or four new piano concertos each season. Since the theater space were limited, he reserving unconventional venues: a large area in the Trattnerhof home, and the ballroom at Mehlgrube's dining establishment. The performances were a hit and the concertos were premiered. in the early 1900s. There are still solid pieces of the collection. Solomon says that during the time, Mozart created "an unified connection between a thrilled composer and an enthusiastic audience who was offered the opportunity of witnessing the transformation and innovation of a key musical genre".

With huge returns from his performances and other locations, Mozart and his partner decided to live in a more luxurious style. They moved into a costly condo or apartment, and the annual rent of about 460 florins. Mozart purchased a magnificent fortepiano made by Anton Walter for about 900 florins and an billiard table at around 300. Mozart and his family Mozarts sent their son Karl Thomas to a costly institution for boarding and also employed servants. Through this time Mozart kept a small portion of his income.

On the 14th of December, 1784 Mozart became a Freemason and was admitted before his lodge Zur Wohltatigkeit (" Beneficence"). Freemasonry played an important role throughout Mozart's existence: he took part in meetings, some of his best acquaintances were Masons as well as on many occasions, he created Masonic songs, e.g. the Maurerische Trauermusik.

1786-1787: Return To Opera

Regardless of the great popular success in Die Entfuhrung aus dem Serail, Mozart did little operatic writing over the next four years, composing only two incomplete works as well as the single-act Der Schauspieldirektor. He remained focused on his work as a musician for the piano and composer of concertos. In 1785, towards the end, Mozart moved from keyboard writing and began his well-known operatic collaboration along with composer Lorenzo Da Ponte. 1786 witnessed the most successful version in the production of The Marriage of Figaro in Vienna. The reception for the opera to Prague at the end of 1787 was warmer, and led to an additional collaboration with Da Ponte. This time it was The opera Don Giovanni, which premiered in the month of October 1787 to great praise in Prague but not much success in Vienna as of 1788. Both are among Mozart's most acclaimed works and constitute the foundation of his an operatic repertoire today, but at their finest, their technical complexity caused a lot of problems for both listeners and entertainers. These developments were not noticed by Mozart's father, who died on May 28th, 1787.

In the month of December 1787 Mozart was eventually granted a regular post with a stylish patronage. The Emperor Joseph II selected him as his "chamber composer" the position that was unoccupied the previous month after the death of Gluck. It was a temporary appointment that paid only 800 florins per year. He also required Mozart only to compose dances for the annual balls at the Redoutensaal (see Mozart and dance). The modest sum was a necessity for Mozart in the midst of difficult times. Court records indicate that Joseph was determined to prevent the well-known composer from moving out of Vienna to search for higher-paying customers.

In 1787, young Ludwig van Beethoven spent some weeks in Vienna in 1787, wishing to learn with Mozart. The absence of reliable evidence makes it difficult to get through to indicate whether the two composers have ever had a conversation.

Chapter 4: Final Years As A Music Industry

At the close of the decade, his circumstances became more difficult. In 1786, he had ceased performing in public concerts, and his earnings decreased. It was a difficult time for musicians in Vienna due to the Austro-Turkish War: both the general level of success as well as the ability of the upper classes to finance music had dwindled.

In the middle of 1788, Mozart and his family were moving from Vienna to the suburbs of Alsergrund. Although it is believed that Mozart tried to cut down on his lease expenses by moving to a more residential area according to his letters addressed to Michael von Puchberg, Mozart did not reduce his expenses however he did increase the amount of real estate at his available. Mozart began to get money, mostly from his close companion and mason Puchberg; "a pitiful series of letters in support of loans" continues to be circulated. Maynard Solomon and others have speculated that Mozart was depressed and that his musical output decreased. Important works from the period include the three symphonies that he composed in the final years (Nos. 39 40, 41 and 39 each dating from 1788) and the final of the three Da Ponte operas Cosi fan tutte was first performed in 1790.

In the same period, Mozart made some long travels to boost his fortunes. He travelled in Leipzig, Dresden, and Berlin in the spring of 1789 as well as Frankfurt, Mannheim, and other German cities in 1790.

1791
Mozart's 2015 was, up until the time his last illness struck, a year of outstanding performance and according to some it was also a time that brought personal

recovery. He composed a wide amount of music, not just a few of his most admired works such as his musical The Magic Flute; the final Piano Concerto (K. 595, in B) and The Clarinet concerto. 622, the final in his string quartets (K. 614 with E) and Motet Ave versum corpus. 618 and the incomplet Requiem K. 626. These were among the finest pieces.

Mozart's financial situation, which was an issue of concern in 1790, was finally beginning to increase. Although the cause isn't clear however, it is believed that wealthy clients in Hungary and Amsterdam offered that they would pay annuities Mozart in exchange for an random structure. The theory is that Mozart profited from the opportunity to sell dance music he composed in his capacity as an Imperial chamber music composer. Mozart did not receive significant sums from Puchberg and began to settle any financial obligation he had.

He was extremely happy with the popularity in a few of his compositions particularly The Magic Flute (which was repeated several times during the short time between the best version and Mozart's passing) as well as the Little Masonic Cantata. 623 which was premiered on the 17th of November in 1791.

His Last Health Issue and Death

Mozart was ill at Prague for the best on the 6th September 1791, from his opera, La clemenza de Tito that was composed in the exact year. It was commissioned for the Emperor's coronation celebrations. He continued his work for a brief period of time and performed his finest in The Magic Flute on 30 September. The health of his body began to decline on the 20th of November, and the musician was bedridden suffering from pain, swelling and vomiting.

Mozart was cared for in his final days by his wife and the youngest sister of her and was assisted by his family physician, Thomas Franz Closset. He was mentally focused on the task of completing his Requiem and the proof that he was able to determine the passages of his pupil Franz Xaver Sussmayr is minimal. [84]

Mozart died in his home on the 5th of December 1791 (aged 35) at 12:55 am. His funeral service in the New Grove defines his funeral ceremony:

Mozart was laid to rest in a typical tomb, which was in line with the modern Viennese custom-designed, in the St. Marx Cemetery outside the city on the 7th of December. If, as the later reports state, there was no funeral service to go to the grave, that is also in accordance with Viennese burial traditions in the period; later Otto Jahn (1856) wrote that Salieri, Sussmayr, van Swieten and two other music artists were present. The story of a snow storm is not true. The day was mild and calm.

The term "typical tomb" refers to neither a typical tomb or a pauper's grave however, it is a tomb that is a unique one for an individual who is a part of the common people (that means, it's not for the upper classes). Most tombs were excavated after 10 years, but the tombs of the aristocratic were not.

The cause of Mozart's death isn't fully understood. The hitziges' authority report Frieselfieber ("extreme military fever" that describes an rash that resembles millet seed) is more of a diagnosis of symptoms rather than a health diagnosis. Scientists have proposed more than 100 causes of death. It includes severe rheumatic disease trichinosis, streptococcal infection and influenza, as well as mercury poisoning and an unusual kidney condition.

Mozart's modest funeral didn't demonstrate his credibility in the eyes of the people as a musician. funerals and concerts held in Vienna as well as Prague were well-loved by the public. It is certain that in the years immediately following his death, his popularity grew dramatically. Solomon describes the term as an "extraordinary surge of enthusiasm" to his works. bios were initially written through Schlichtegroll, Niemetschek, and Nissen Publishers fought to publish full editions of his work.

Chapter 5: His Personality And His Character

The appearance of Mozart's physique was described by the tenor Michael Kelly in his Reminiscences: "an incredibly little man very light and thin, sporting an abundant amount of fine, fair hair, of which he was quite a bit egocentric". His first biographer Niemetschek said "there was nothing special about his body. ... He was small and his face aside from his large, extreme eyes did not show any signs of his talent." The skin of his face was pitted and swollen, suggesting a childhood smallpox. In regards to his voice, his wife later said that he "was an tenor that was delicate in speech and fragile when singing, however, when anything enticed him or was the result of having to be applied and it worked, it was powerful and full of energy."

He was a fan of elegant clothes. Kelly remembers him from the wedding rehearsal" He was standing on stage in his crimson pelisse as well as a gold-laced cocked-hat, giving the timing of the orchestra's music." Based on photographs that scientists had the capability of locating of Mozart and his wig, he was seen to be wearing a white hairdo throughout his formal occasions. scientists from the Salzburg Mozarteum revealed that only one of the 14 photos they discovered were shown the man without his hair.

Mozart generally worked for a long time and was a hard worker and completed structures in a staggeringly fast pace when due dates came closer. He usually sketched and drafts, but in contrast to Beethoven's, they were not kept up to date since his co-workers was determined to ruin them following his death.

Mozart was at the very center of the Viennese music scene, and he knew a large number in a wide range of individuals, including fellow performers, theatrical entertainers as well as colleagues, Salzburgers and aristocrats not just certain associates of the Emperor Joseph II. Solomon thinks that his three most best friends to be Gottfried von Jacquin and the Count August Hatzfeld, and Sigmund Barisani. Other friends include his principal associate Joseph Haydn, vocalists Franz Xaver Gerl and Benedikt Schack, and musician Joseph Leutgeb. Leutgeb and Mozart played a wacky kind of mockery that was friendly, mostly using Leutgeb as the nastiest of Mozart's jokes.

He was a fan of dancing, billiards and also kept animals this includes a canary, an eagle as well as a pet dog and an animal for leisure riding. He had an enthralling love for scatological humor, which remains in his long-running letters, including those for his sister Maria Anna Thekla Mozart around 1777-1778, as well as in his correspondence with his parents and sister. Mozart also wrote music scatological which included a number of canons which he sang with his best friends. Mozart was raised as a Catholic and remained a faithful religious member throughout his lifetime.

Chapter 6: The Style And The Simple Ness Of His Character

Mozart's music, as well as Haydn's, is an ideal model for classical music. Classical style. In the period he was writing, European music was controlled by the galant style in response to the complex and highly developed style of the Baroque. Gradually, and in large part, due to Mozart himself the intricate contrapuntal complexities that were characteristic of late Baroque returned controlled and moderated through new arrangements and adapted to a different social and visual scene. Mozart was a flex composer who composed in all the major categories which included but not limited to symphony opera, solo concerto, chamber works composed of string quartets and string quintet, as well as the sonata for piano. The forms are not brand original however Mozart enhanced their technical elegance and psychological resemblance.

He essentially created and promoted Classical Piano Concerto. He composed a lot of music for the spiritual, this includes huge masses, as well as music for dance, divertimenti, serenades as well as other forms of entertainment for the home. [

The primary traits characteristic of that Classical style are evident within Mozart's compositions. Clarity, balance and openness are the hallmarks of his music however, the simplest ideas of its uniqueness conceal the extraordinary quality of his most acclaimed works of art, such as Mozart's Piano Concerto No. 24, in C smaller, K. 491; the Symphony No. 40 G smaller, K. 550; and the opera Don Giovanni. Charles Rosen makes the point with a powerful voice:

It is only by acknowledging the violence and sensuality that lie at the heart of Mozart's music that we can gain understanding his compositions and gain a better understanding of the greatness of his work. In a strange way, Schumann's superficial characterisation of the G small

Symphony will help us discover the daemon in Mozart's work more gradually. In all Mozart's greatest expressions of terror and pain there's something incredibly sensual.

In his final decennium Mozart frequently abused chromatic consistency. An example of this can be found in his String Quartet in C significant K. 465 (1785) which's intro is abundant in chromatic suspensions, which led to its name as the "Dissonance" group.

Mozart had a knack for absorbing and adapting the vital aspects of music from other composers. His travels contributed to the development of a distinct music language. In London as a youngster the composer was introduced to J. C. Bach and was exposed to his music. Then, in Paris, Mannheim, and Vienna there were additional compositional influences and the ability to evolve in Mannheim's orchestra. Mannheim orchestra. In Italy He encountered the Italian overture and the opera buffa that both profoundly affected the development of his technique. Within London and Italy the style of galant was popular of the day: simple light music, with the fervor for cadencing, the emphasis was on dominant, tonic and subdominant in the absence of other consistency; symmetrical expressions; and clearly articulated sections in the general shape of the movements. A few of Mozart's earliest symphonies are Italian overtures, having three movements that run in one another; some are homotonal (all three movements share the same fundamental signature, with only the slow middle movement remaining smaller). Some of them are a recreation of the work composed by J. C. Bach while others demonstrate the simple binary structures that were developed with Viennese composers.

As Mozart became more sophisticated, he slowly introduced more functions that were more abridged to the Baroque. Here's an example: in the Symphony No. 29 from A Major K. It has the contrapuntal theme as its principal theme in its opening movement, as well as an experiment using a variety of lengths for expressions. Certain of his quartets composed in 1773 feature fugal endings that were likely influenced by Haydn who had included three such closings in his newly launched Opus twenty set. The effect on this Sturm und Drang (" Storm and Tension") period of music, and its brief foreshadowing of the Romantic period, is evident in the music composed by both composers of the time. Mozart's Symphony No. Twenty-five with G minor K. Another outstanding instance.

Mozart could at times shift his focus from operas to critical music. He wrote operas in each of the dominant styles such as opera buffa, such as The Marriage of Figaro, Don Giovanni, and Cosi fan tutte, opera seria, such as Idomeneo and Singspiel which of Die Zauberflote is the most famous example of any composer. In his later works, he made subtle adjustments to orchestral texture, instrumentation and tone color, to provide psychological depth and to signal major changes. The advances in the field of opera and critical composition were communicated through his increasingly sophisticated orchestral use in concertos and symphonies had an impact on his orchestration in operas and the development of his subtlety of orchestra use to affect the mind during his operas was in the later structures that were not operatic.

Mozart composed music that anyone can understand: It's simple beautiful, breathtaking, and a perfect solution to our busy lives. Right? But not too quick. An analyst Rob Kapilow says it's simple to break the Mozart bubble.

" If you study the critics of Mozart's day they're always saying this music was meant suitable for intellectuals of 5 or 6 years old. It's astonishing: This is the best that we have, yet in the time of Mozart it was considered to be professional, intellectual and expert's music." Kapilow says.

For a good example of Mozart's false simplicity, Kapilow identifies a passage from the String Quintet in G small K. 516. It's a work that he describes as one of Mozart's most extraordinary. On the piano Kapilow illustrates how the music seen on the surface of an effortless musical expression doesn't tell the complete picture.

" First Kapilow is breaking our illusion that this is a simple four-bar movement," Kapilow says. The four steps sound secure at first however, later Mozart expands the expression. He duplicates, but alters elements that the melody possesses in a variety of ways, including overlapping and transferring expressions to various instruments. However, after all the complexity, Kapilow says, Mozart is able to retool the theme to make it sound simpler.

" It's a bit like a hologram" Kapilow says. "On one hand, when the surface appears simple but there is something subtlely subversive and unstable underneath that is that is stabilizing it. However, if the surface appears complicated it's because there's a fantastic basic, symmetrical balance that is reflected underneath. That's what makes Mozart's music so wonderful."

After their deaths artists are a victim of the past. The ones who get through are those who can be flexible and are able to take on the changing waves of idealistic visions, ideology and theories, styles and disaster that comprise the current zeitgeist. The ones who survive, however, are not always able to ride these waters without incident. Two instances to consider can be JS Bach as well as Mozart. Bach was conceived by the time of his generation, however, he he was not able to outlast the time; Mozart was well-in tune with his age but his legacy was reinterpreted in subsequent generations.

The thing that most was the most important thing that made Bach to become Bach was the family tradition of composers passing generations as well as it was the Lutheran church, where music was interspersed into services. Bach became an Lutheran composer during the peak of the baroque era which was a period that was a time of extravagant, lavishly decorated music and architecture. Through the latter half of his professional career the baroque style was pave the way for the brightness and elegance of the classical style in its early stages and quickly morphed into becoming the high-classical style of Mozart as well as Haydn. To add to the posthumous defamation that was being hurled at us, the most prominent singers of the younger generation included JS Bach's Sons WF, JC (a coach to Mozart) and CPE. These sons honored their father and kept his name in the public domain, however within their own circle, they called him "the old Wig".

It was the dawning of the classical spirit that prompted one of the most well-known bad reviews, published in 1737 by a former Bach pupils JA Scheibe." Bach could win the love of all nations when he was more charming and didn't take away the natural element from his work by creating an unnatural and disorganized style, and did not dim their appeal with an excess in art." The new zeitgeist's definition of to be "natural" was awe-inspiring and easy to hear and popular. It was quasi-artless, fast-paced, and pleasing, perhaps.

Contrary to the myths of later times, Bach was always remembered before his revival in 19th century, however the public adored him more than he played. It is interesting that the charge of "an over-the-top art" and used to attack Bach when he was in his early years of 2015, was a charge that plagued Mozart throughout his maturation.

The famous issue with Emperor Joseph II regarding The Marriage of Figaro - "a many note, Mozart" There are a lot of notes, Mozart. It is often interpreted as an oversight by an uninformed blockhead. In reality, Joseph was echoing what nearly everyone, even his admirers, had to say about Mozart his genius: Mozart was so imaginative that he was unable to stop it and that led to his music becoming extremely, and even demon-like. This is why Mozart's negative or perhaps even sour, judgments: "too highly spiced"; "impenetrable mazes"; "strange thoughts of the soul"; "overloaded and overstuffed".

In final, esteem of Mozart at his time was as it is now He was seen as an unbeatable master. In the time that Beethoven arrived to Vienna on 1792 zeitgeist of music was outlined through Haydn in addition to Mozart. If Beethoven was rooted in their culture, a classicist by nature, the setting surrounding his was Romantic. If you're a thought-provoking and politically modernist, Beethoven was your guy. Although he was not a Romantic but he was the definitive composer for Romantics and was the primary driver for the coming. The musical ties to the rest of the century and the past were, most importantly Beethoven's.

On the other hand certainly Beethoven isn't any higher on the scale of awe than the long ignored Bach. Beethoven's status was granted at the time of his birth. The time of his birth created the famous cult of genius. Romantics needed divinities. From his inexplicably skilled and his shrewd style, to his extravagant suffering and perseverance of his own existence, Beethoven is a perfect fit for the part of the Romantic hero. He would not have had the chance to play the role in the event that the time had not created the character around his character.

This brings us back to Mozart The incredibly devil to the great musicians of his day who did well, but in a unique way during the Romantic century. In the present, adjectives and nouns were vastly different than in his time: "tranquility, repose, grace," said Schumann; "his good-natured and healthy personality,"" stated Tchaikovsky; "sweet sunlight," declared Dvorak. Incredibly that, the Romantic Zeitgeist was a time of transcendence sky-scraping and world-changing massively suffering. The whole thing pushed Mozart towards the left. He was according to the saying"the Dresden porcelain doll for composers.

In settlement, Mozart's story and death were rewritten into Romantic legends: Mozart the was misinterpreted, the unnoticed and the poor. Actually, he earned a great deal of money, and was thought to be the greatest composer of his time. Yet, Romantics, and modernists following them, had to think that the genius of their time is often viewed as unimportant, misinterpreted and so on.

. In the past few years, only the dark aspect of Mozart was discovered by directors and viewers recognizing that, for example, even with all the fun and slapstick, Don Giovanni is as sexually sexy and groovy as the man who wrote it. What's the reason for this re-discovery? We're all the beneficiaries of postmodernism and modernism. We are awed by those who are dark and absurd and transgressive - the entire teen virtues. In the days of Mozart's critics, they threw down their arms in disapproval of Don Giovanni, calling it immoral and impious - and they were correct. But today these are the qualities that make us enthralled. It is now Mozart's style, grace and wit that be overlooked.

The study of research into artists and zeitgeists may be ongoing since it's a dialectic that continues to be a constant in historical time. The story goes on to explain how the poor saps of history alters out. This includes Luigi Cherubini, in France loved by all through Marie

Antoinette through Napoleon to the Bourbon repair, Beethoven's most favored modern composer, but now is a footnote. It's amazing that out of the many 10s of musicians who have achieved great success throughout their careers Some have the capacity to endure the rigors of the past and not fall. It's a wonder that everyone can relate to.

Mozart was profoundly influenced by the changing political, social and philosophical climate of his day and this is evident through the subversive notes of his music and his actions.

Mozart The Freelancer

At the age of 17, Mozart was already an accomplished artist, and was appointed as the composer of the court for his archbishop in Salzburg. It was certain that this would result in the disputes Mozart faced with two of the most authoritative people in his life who were his authority figures The Archbishop, who would try to hinder and scold Mozart for a long time after the time he resigned of the Court; as well as father Leopold who was the autocrat in charge of Mozart's young genius.

These conflicts would create significant concern to Mozart within his Salzburg post and also in relationships with father. The archbishop's demands restricted the range of his plans. With a variety of courtly commissionsincluding symphonies, dances and quartets, he couldn't pursue the things he wanted to create: opera. This situation, coupled with the embarrassingly small pay he earned was enough to force Mozart to take a sensible decision but, in a way unexpected: He quit.

The decision to be a judge was exciting however it would be just the beginning of his dispute against the archbishop. The ultimate decision could be the first of his many disputes with his father. However, it also led to the beginning of a revolution for Mozart.

The composers of the 1800s typically were paid commissions from dukes, kings and other nobles with money to spend. Composers would be paid to compose works of a large size like symphonies, requiems, or requi or an annual salary. The value of these works was attributed to the nobles simply because they improved the reputation of clients as people of high taste and money.

For the good of Mozart but there were plenty of other possibilities of success that were surfacing for Mozart. Opera is, although always a major source of entertainment has now become a famous and profitable business. A growing number of people had the option of paying to go to the theatre, and since the class of middle-class of cities like Vienna was growing, so did their appetite for musical theater. Operas, as big-scale productions, were supported by wealthy citizens who saw huge financial investment for what was to come for the theatre in the near future.

Mozart's father was firmly against his earning money through freelance work. He was even more insistent on his child be prevented from doing so in Vienna in a city in a city where he was not restricted. In his turn the Archbishop continued to stop Mozart's attempts to work beyond the established limits of the court from which he gone, then returned, and tried to leave the court again. Mozart was a bizarre phenomenon. He was known as the most feisty musician in Europe.

Slamming Upper class

Mozart's defiance of convention was just beginning however. He was openly questioned due to his status as an artist of immense genius who was a child in his conduct and how he used money. His public Image however was a distant memory in comparison to the arguments that were a part of his work--in particular, two of his most popular and deeply-rooted operas: The Marriage of Figaro and Don

Giovanni. Both can be described as Knowledge period pieces, affected by issues that were essential to the time including the role of the higher class and sexual liberties.

Both of the operas target upper-class people in a significant way, perhaps not so surprising considering the time period they were written in. The decade of 1780s can be described as a perfect blend of the American and the Reign Of Terrors. The extraordinary acts of rebellion flipped the order of power in their specific societies. They no longer needed to be submissive to the rule of the nobility, or the upper class. The two plays Figaro along with Don Giovanni call out nobles who abuse their power and show ordinary people who struggle and eventually triumph despite their oppressors.

Despite all his critique of the power elite It is still appealing to note that Mozart's works did not weaken or shook up any authority. In the end great thinkers like

Rousseau and Locke were laying the foundations for the current political system of the time for several years at this time. However, there is a distinct distinction between the work of thought-leaders and the operas composed by Mozart. Authors who published works like Rousseau might be at risk of being punished severely by authorities, even though The Marriage of Figaro was orchestrated by and performed by the Emperor Joseph II of Austria. To stage an opera even with censorship and then still proclaim its authority as being flawed--and doing it in front of the Emperor was a clever way to deflect every obnoxious character in Mozart's world.

A Warning for the future

The romantic and sexual relationships that are featured in these operas convey the same message. The villains in the two operettas Don Giovanni and Count Almaviva pursue women they are aware of are tied to males and assault anyone of a less privileged class than themselves. The most significant thematic distinction however, occurs at the final scene of both operas. Don Giovanni, unrepentant and brave in the face of his inevitable doom, gets forced towards Hell. The story is based on The Marital relationship of Figaro however, the Count reconciles with his partner, allowing the marriage to last with a true "happily always after" in the final scene.

The intended audience of the two operas could be defined as any group of people, depending on which aspect of each one you decide to study. They represent the members from the class of workers, those who, just like Mozart are able to thrive in any circumstance either beneficial or not. They also proclaim certain freedoms from tyranny declaring to humane kings as well as exuberant emperors alike what they thought for a long time "No further!" The starkly divergent outcomes of both operas prove this. Mozart provides a model of what might befall those who are in charge when they push their limits to the limit: repentance, an opportunity to retake the reins or even a final damnation to Hell.

How do we think about this?

Don't fall for the humorous version of Mozart as depicted by the well-known 1984 film, Amadeus. The man was not a fool (immature perhaps, but certainly not stupid). He understood the ability of art to influence the opinions of the public at large and understood how the winds in politics of the time were transforming. His work, and especially his operas, provide a record of the dynamic and informed thought about the time.

Chapter 7: The Grand Tour 1763-66

"Just like how people behave towards me, I also act towards them. If I observe that someone hates myself and treats me with disdain I'm as proud as a peacock."
WOLFGANG AMADEUS MOZART

After these short excursions, Leopold Mozart decided that it was the right time to introduce Mozart, the world's most famous child prodigy, to the art of traveling, and he decided to embark on a lengthy trip of three years across Europe. In the following three years Mozart performed in 17 cities across seven different countries.

Leopold Mozart wanted to begin the tour as soon as he could so that he could make the most of their youthful years and the potential of their talents. Wolfgang was seven at the time of the tour, while Nannerl aged eleven. The itinerary included southern Germany as well as The Austrian Netherlands (i.e., Belgium), Paris,

Switzerland and possibly northern Italy as well as Rome. The London section was added in the wake of several influential Englishmen had pressured him in Paris and the stopping point in the Netherlands was completely unplanned. The plan was to bring into as numerous European courts as is possible and also the major cultural capitals as per the tradition in the Grand Tour.

There were many things to be planneddue to the volatile nature of royal courts as well as their ability to pay for all sorts of things. It was likely that payment would occur however Leopold did not have the right to demand an amount in a certain amount and often, payment came by way of an expensive object, like an expensive snuff box made of gold. While these items could have been to an aspiring teenager, these were actually a form of payment of some kind, and they enriched Leopold tremendously. Leopold is a determined person, as was his spouse Anna Maria deferred to him despite her fierce determination. Anna Maria was not a fan of the tour due to the fact that Wolfgang was unwell during the few tour they took in prior to the year, but she was supportive of his decision.

Leopold was, for his part was dependent on his professional network of musicians and the connections to social networks he'd established prior to the smaller tours to get invitations from numerous royal courts. Leopold had the help of his trusted friends Johann Lorenz Hagenauer, the landlord as well as business partner and close friend of Leopold. Hagenauer was a prominent trader with numerous connections across Europe and provided an arrangement of banks that allowed them to get money from various cities, while waiting for payments from different royal families. He also asked his employer the Prince, Archbishop of Salzburg to be granted an extended leave of absence. The leave was granted despite the fact that Hagenauer was only appointed vice-Kapellmeister in the month of January

1763. This was because it could bring honor to Salzburg and to the Archbishop, Prince, as well as to God.

Young Wolfgang was a fervent student of the harpsichord. According to his memories from his father and his sister the violinist honed his playing technique on the violin without receiving any instruction from anyone. The two kids composed several duets that they could perform and clearly enjoyed creating music with each other.

In the previous year, Leopold had managed to save the equivalent of two years' worth of salary as vice-Kapellmeister in the course of his trip to Vienna in the year before, and used the funds to fund the trip.

First Stop Munich

T
the family set off June 9th, 1763 in the carriage they purchased the previous year.

However, on the first day, a wheel fell off which forced them to stay for one day at Wasserburg-am-Inn as it was being fixed. Leopold used the delay to take Wolfgang to the local church where he introduced the child into the church organ. They made it to Munich shortly after, and went on to perform four concerts during June, featuring Mozart and Nannerl performing together in each of them and in front of the Elector Maximilian III. One of the shows took place on the night 13th June 1763 from 8 o'clock to 11 o'clock at night. These performances earned the family around 200 florins.

Augsburg

A
After achieving great success following a great run Munich After a long and successful stay in Munich, the family left on June 22 1763 to Augsburg in Germany, which is where Leopold had many connections since the place he was born and spent his childhood there. Leopold's

mom, from whom he had a discordant relationship and who was unable to go to any of the performances. In the early years, Wolfgang was still a young boy who was home sick often waking up at night, crying, and naming specific people from Salzburg whom he did not see. The family also staged three concerts for the public in Augsburg before moving to the town of Schwetzingen that was the seat for the legendary Mannheim court, which was home to the most prestigious orchestras in Europe. Mannheim was the location in which the first orchestras formed and the symphony was invented. In Mannheim, the Electors Palatine Karl Theodor and his electress were awestruck.

Frankfurt

F
After the visit to following the stop at Mannheim court The family then went to Frankfurt-am-Main. Leopold wrote about the concerts on the 20th of August 1763:

"We performed an evening concert on the 18th of November that was extraordinary. Everyone was amazed. We are so blessed to be well and, wherever we go, we are is admired. In the case of little Wolfgangerl the kid is very playful, however, he is also quite reckless. Little Nannerl is no longer his shadow and is now playing with such skill that the world speaks of her and is amazed by her."

It's a shocking admission given the role of women in the world in the period when both children were given equal treatment.

At Frankfurt, Mozart gave a solo performance, announcing it with all the swagger that is expected from an ebullient father. In the advertisement of the Frankfurt newspaper said:

"He Wolfgang" will play an arrangement for violin, as well as accompanying orchestras on the harpsichord. When he is doing this you will cover the piano in an apron, and the young Mozart will play as easily as if he were able to see the keys. He will immediately identify all notes played from the distance, either singly or in chords like on the harpsichord, or any other instrument like a bell, glass or clock. In the end, he will play improvised on both the harpsichord as well as the organ for as long as he wishes or in any note."

In Frankfurt the famous author Johann Wolfgang von Goethe, who was then 14 years old was present at a performance given by the two children, and they were compensated the sum of four Gulden and 7 Kreuzers for the privilege. Johann Peter Eckermann later spoke with Goethe about the meeting. He wrote:
"I saw him,""
said Goethe,
"at seven years old," when he performed a show when we were on our way. I was around 14 years old, and I still remember perfectly the tiny man, sporting his frissure and sword. Rarely, a phenomenon as rare as Mozart's Mozart remains an utterly inexplicable phenomenon."
Goethe's description of Mozart is quite accurate. In the future, however Goethe

did compare Mendelssohn positively to Mozart and claimed that he possessed the same look and feel as Mozart in the way that a conversation from an adult man is similar to his "prattle of a toddler."

Smaller Centers

T
The family then made the cruise ship that took them to Koblenz, Bonn, and Cologne. It's not clear whether they were in any of these smaller cities however, they did travel westwards towards Aachen and did a show for the princess Anna Amalia of Prussia, the sister of Frederick the Great of Prussia. Princess Anna Amalia tried to convince Leopold to resign from his tour and travel towards Berlin in order to play for Frederick the Great however Leopold refused to go.

Following Aachen and Aachen, the family travelled to Mainz and hoped to entertain the elector. Unfortunately, the Elector was sick, and their family decided to perform three concerts in public, to which they received 200 Gudens.

In the beginning of the month of September, 1763 they arrived in Koblenz which is where Leopold wrote, incredulously to Hagenauer:
"We do not have any relationships with aristocrats, and other prestigious people. Honestly!"

Brussels

T
The family moved to Brussels on the 4th of October and the family stayed there in Brussels for six months. Leopold addressed his acquaintance Hagenauer:
"We were at Brussels during three weeks and then Prince Karl [of Lorraine Governor of the Austrian Netherlands] himself spoke to me and stated that he would like to meet my children in the next few days, but there has been no sign of it. Indeed, it appears like nothing is going to happen because the Prince has no intention of

hunting or gorge himself on booze and, in the end it is revealed that he is not able to pay. As of now I've not been able, despite my respect for my manners, to leave or perform a show, as according to the instructions of the Prince I have to wait for whether he would make a decision."

In the midst of this pause in Brussels waiting for the Prince's decision to stop his hunt Wolfgang was composing. On October 14 Wolfgang composed his Allegro for harpsichord. It would later be integrated in the C major sonata K. 6, which was completed in Paris.

Leopold's desire to perform for Prince Karl seems to have been fulfilled, for they gave a concert on November 9th, 1763, that was reported on the Augspurgische Ordinari-Post-Zeitung on December 12th, 1763:
"What was reported to us in July by the Electoral Court of the Palatinate and later in August and September , from Frankfurt, Mainz, and the Electoral Court in Trier

with so many expressions of awe that we believed to be unbelievable, then certainly exaggerated. We have been awestruck by the incredible skill of the two sons from Herr Leopold Mozart, vice-Kapellmeister at the Most Serene court in Salzburg known for his compositions, and the publication of his exquisite Violin-Schule. On the 9th day of November, this month an extravagant concert was held at the Salle du Concert Bourgeois, and was attended not only by a number of nobles as well as His Royal His Royal Duke Carl himself. They everyone was filled with indescribable joy."

"Now these delightful children (who are singular) have travelled across the world to Paris."

Paris Success

T
He set off for Paris France on November 15th which was the capital of classical music of the time. He arrived in Paris on

the 18th of November, 1763. They spent the next five months at Paris over five months. They were located in the Hotel Beauvais in the rue St Antoine in the residence of the Count Maximilian Emanuel Franz von Eyck who was who was the Bavarian Ambassador. The Mozarts arrived in Paris with a number of letters of recommendation from the nobles and aristocratic patrons, but none gave them the audience they desired, with the exception of one they received from Friedrich Melchior Grimm, given to them by the wife of a famous Frankfurt businessman. Grimm was a former resident of Paris and was involved in a variety of artist conflicts that raged during the 1760s and 70s which included the well-known Querelle des Bouffons, which created Italian comedy in Paris. Grimm also made the decision to take the family to his home because of the incredible reviews they received about their work. In the wake of this prayer the family relocated to Versailles on December 24, and on January 1, 1764, they gave the concert to Louis XV. On one particular occasion, while Mozart was having dinner alongside the Queen, Mozart stood beside her and kissed her hand as she fed him bits of food. The Mozarts fame predated them and they were celebrated by the nobility everywhere they were.

In Versailles The couple made an effort to visit the famous Versailles. They also visited the famous mistress of the King Madame de Pompadour, who was an old lady at the time, even though she was, as per Leopold,
"an extremely sexually agressive woman who was still the king of all matters."
According to Nannerl's later memories, Wolfgang was forced to stand on a stool and undergo an examination in the presence of Madame de Pompadour, and she refused to let him kiss her.

There is no evidence of the children performing a formal performance at Versailles. On February 17, 1764, the children received fifty dollars (about 560 florins) and a gold snuff box by the entertainments department of the royal family. The unusual payment is believed to be a way to entertain the royal family at home however, no other details are available. The Mozarts gave private, exclusive performances at Paris between March 10, and 9th of April at a theater situated in Porte St. Honore.

Grimm wrote that the young Wolfgang was
"so remarkable a phenomenon one can't believe until one has witnessed the man in person and heard him in your own ears."
While Mozart composed the Allegro movement for the KV 6 sonata for violin and harpsichord at Brussels in the midst of waiting for Karl to appear to compose it, he finished the piece in Paris along with three more sonatas for violin and harpsichord KV 7/8 and 9, while the composer was just seven years old. young. (KV refers to Kochelverzeichnis the index of Mozart's entire works composed in the hands of Ludwig von Kochel.)

Leopold decided to have them printed and engraved in Paris and also to publish them in Paris, despite the fact the author was a seven year old boy. The boy enjoyed watching as they sold out the first edition.

When he was in Paris, Nannerl was compared with the best virtuosos the time, however young Wolfgang was awed by his skills on the piano or violin as well as organ. He was also not content to listen to the arias of Italian as well as French operas, but he would also perform them on the spot for an audience. He also created an improvised accompaniment to a cavatina's bassline he didn't even have a clue about. He also started a sequence of improvisations which were complete works. He could create brand new compositions on demand to the delight of French audience. He was a cult figure in Versailles.

Mozart had a meeting with the great Mannheim Harpsichordist and composer

Johann Schobert, who went around spouting admonitions regarding the young musician in the back of his back, much to the annoyance of Leopold who wrote about this behavior in his letter to friend Hagenauer. Mozart also dated and became friends with one of the Augsburg native composer Johann Gottfried Eckhardt. It was apparent that musical compositions from the Mannheim school, particularly Johann Stamitz was very popular as were other composers, Franz Joseph Haydn, and Johann Christian Bach were being extensively performed and published also.

After Paris the family departed for Calais on the 10th of April, 1764. They arrived in London on the 23rd April 1764.

London

T
he first place the Mozarts lived in London was in Cecil Court, near St. Martin-in-the-Fields, above a barbershop. They had

invitation letters from Paris that served them extremely well. In fact, just four days following their arrival to London they performed for the King George III and his young German queen, Charlotte Sophia. Their performance was so popular that they were instantly scheduled to return on May 19th. In this performance, the King asked him to play pieces composed by Handel, Johann Christian Bach and Carl Friedrich Abel. He also joined the Queen while she sang an aria. Later when he was improvising on the bass line from the Handel aria.

Leopold did his best to secure performances in the name of the Mozart children. And considering that many of the gentry and nobility of England were expected to leave the city for summer He also realized that the majority of them returned on June 4, the birthday of the King which is why he planned the concert on the 5th of June. After the huge success of the concert, he aimed to secure Wolfgang an invitation to the charity concert of the maternity hospital on the 29th of June at the Ranelagh Pleasure Gardens. Leopold rightly noted that the English loved charitable events and believed that this would be a good way to introduce him towards the English.

Wolfgang was described as
"the famed and amazing master Mozart", a young child seven years old"
even though he was only at the age of eight. The notice continued to say that he was
"justly is regarded as the most remarkable prodigy, and the most astounding genius to have been seen in any time."

Just a week later Mozart was performing in a private concert in The Grosvenor Square home of the Earl of Thanet. Following the performance, Leopold returned home with an inflammation of the throat, as well as other signs of acute. Leopold himself believed that he was dying, and wrote to his friend Hagenauer. Hagenauer "prepare your heart to be awash with one of the most tragic incidents."

In actual fact, he was in fact, sick for several weeks, and during that the children could not perform. The family relocated into the countryside, and eventually to the 180 Ebury Street in Pimlico (which was then a distinct town, not part of the city of London like it is today!)

Wolfgang would spend his time writing music in this period since the musician was not able to perform. Sometime during this time and in England, Mozart met Johann Christian Bach and was prompted to compose the symphonies. In any event Mozart wrote his first symphony while awaiting the period of recovery for his father. The symphony is in E flat major KV. 16. His First Symphony is rudimentary by the standards of his later works however it's very much like J. C. Bach. He also began to compose his second symphony (KV 19) in D major, but this was finished at The Hague, later. While these are the only orchestral works written in the period however, there is plenty of evidence that suggests Mozart was thinking orchestrally frequently during this time. There are a few sketches that remain unfinished, which suggest that there might be other symphonies Mozart did not finish and that he wrote during this period.

Alongside the symphonies mentioned above, Mozart composed the piano sonata KV 19d with four hand parts in C major KV 19d. It was and a set of violin sonatas, with additional flute and 'cello pieces and were dedicated upon her request to the Queen Charlotte and then given to her in the month of January 1765. Mozart also composed an aria called "God refuses to be our God" KV 20 as well as an one-time tenor song called "VA, the furor portata" KV 21.

In September, after Leopold recovered Leopold's health, the family relocated to London and moved to the 20th floor of Thrift Street (later renamed Frith Street) located in Soho. The flat was near many concert halls as well as the residences of Johann Christian Bach, the son of Johann Sebastian Bach and music master to the queen as well as Carl Friedrich Abel. Bach became a friend of the family and played music alongside Mozart as a partner. Abel may not have ever met Mozart but Mozart definitely had a good understanding of his symphonies when he attended the Bach-Abel annual concert series.

On the 25th of October On the 25th of October, King George III invited the two children to join him at the celebrations to mark King George III's fourth birthday. Then they were not allowed to perform publicly (they continued to play for private occasions) up to February 21st 1765. It wasn't a spectacular performance, since it was in the same concert in one of Bach's Abel concert which was a shocking mistake on the part Mozart's father. Mozart. But, Leopold reported that
"At each court we've been able to say that we've been greeted with awe however,

what we've seen in England surpasses all others."

The Mozarts gave the chance to listen to Mozart perform in his private accommodation at a cost of five shillings. Mozart would give private performances between April and June 1765. The Mozarts also gave at a concert for the public on May 13th. In June 1765 the two "young Prodigies" performed every day at the Swan and Harp Tavern in Cornhill at a cost of two shillings or sixpence. The shows were planned and the work load of the musicians of the youth was that they had to work hard to pay the expenses incurred due to the lack of money due to Leopold's illness and the high medical costs. According to Leopold said his son Wolfgang continued to grow as an artist, and was impressed by the talent of his youngest son. In light of this, it was somewhat sad that Mozart was regarded as a freak show. Mozarts were considered something of an oddity, like a sort of show that was a freak in London. In true English manner, Mozart was examined by the Honourable Daines Barrington, a renowned scientist, to assess his talents. Barrington found that Mozart was a genius of a different kind. Before leaving for Europe on the 24th July, 1765 Leopold gave the music score of "God is our refuge" for the British Museum.

The Netherlands

W
When the family returned to the continent the family was not in good health. It seems that the weather in England wasn't ideal for them , as Wolfgang was diagnosed with tonsillitis, and Leopold suffered from frequent dizziness attacks. They were compelled to stay for one month in the tiny city of Lille. Though their initial goal was to go back to Paris However, their various illnesses made them reconsider their plans. Leopold was convinced by an envoy from princess Carolina who was Princess Carolina of Orange-Nassau to

travel into The Hague as official guests of the court.

The first week of September, after the entire family was recovering somewhat the family moved to Ghent which is where Wolfgang played on the organ that was just installed in Bernardine's chapel and then a few days later that, he performed at the cathedral organ in Antwerp. The family arrived at the capital city, The Hague, on September 11th 1765.

In the event of luck Nannerl was diagnosed with a severe illness and was unable to perform for the first week of the festival or to perform before she was to perform for the Prince of Orange within a couple of days. But, Leopold was certain enough that Nannerl was able to recover and put the notice for an event that was scheduled to be held on September 30th 1765 in The hall at the Oude Doelen in The Hague. The notice was published in the local newspaper which said:

"All the overtures will come composed by the young composer. [...] Music lovers can be able to confront him with any song at any time and he'll perform it upon the sight of."

There is no record that the concert has ever been held in the first place, and it's almost certain that Nannerl didn't perform due to her the illness of typhoid fever. It was deemed to be so severe that she was treated with extreme unction on the 21st of October The family was able to been able to accept this loss after the doctor of the royal court, Thomas Schwenke intervened and assisted her in recovering at the close of October. The family was shocked when Wolfgang began to fall ill, and didn't recover until the middle of December. The board was put over his bed so it would allow him to continue writing.

It seems that the concert scheduled for September actually occurred on the 22nd of January, 1766. It is probable that it was the first Mozart's Symphony in D (KV 19) and perhaps a brand new Symphony in B-flat major KV 22, that was written while the composer waited for Nannerl to recover. Following this concert, they were well-known throughout the Netherlands and travelled into Amsterdam to stay for two weeks during which they played two sold-out performances on the 29th of January and 26th February 1766. The music was composed of music for instruments composed by Wolfgang's original compositions, before return the following month to The Hague in early March.

The group returned back to The Hague to participate in the "coming of old age" ceremony to honor Prince of Orange. Prince of Orange. Mozart composed an anthem of well-known Dutch songs (called"quodlibet") "quodlibet") named "Gallimathias Musicum" (KV 32) for small orchestras and harpsichord , which was first performed in an exclusive concert in honor of the prince on the 11th of March, 1766. It is interesting to note that Mozart composed several arias to the princess using the libretto for Artaserse which was composed by Metastasio, who was the most well-known Italian librettist in the opera the seria (this is the name used for the most serious Italian Classical operas) and a collection of keyboard variations of the famous Dutch song dubbed "Laat ons juichen Matavieren!" (KV 24) The world's most famous national anthem, as well as the national anthem of The Republic of The Netherlands. Although he was only a few years old, Mozart was a facile and quick composer. He composed a number of sonatas for violin and keyboard dedicated to the princes similar to what he composed to the French princess and queen of England. While in Holland Mozart also composed another symphony (KV 45a) that is now known by the name of "Old Lambach" due to the fact that it was believed to be composed in Lambach Abbey in Austria. Lambach Abbey in Austria in 1679.

Leopold was extremely impressed by the money-making cow the children turned out to be. Leopold instead of heading back to his home town of Salzburg He took them in the month of March 1766 to other towns in The Netherlands, including Haarlem where the organist from St. Bavo's Church invited Mozart to play the most powerful organ in the nation. The group continued to travel from the east and south, playing performances at Amsterdam as well as Utrecht in April. They following across Brussels and Valenciennes before heading to Paris. They arrived on the 10th of May.

The Final Leg of the Tour: Paris, Switzerland and Germany

In Paris They resided at the residence of Grimm, the Bavarian Ambassador, Grimm and he noted how both young people had grown tremendously over the years however, audiences were less enthusiastic when they were no longer young. They nevertheless were on stage at Versailles as well as for the princess of Orleans who presented young Wolfgang with a song she composed herself. The music was also presented to the Crown prince Karl Wilhelm Ferdinand of Brunswick who had achieved an amazing good fortune in his time during the Seven Years War. The Mozarts were extremely impressed with the man, as he was an extremely skilled violinist and was very fascinated by Leopold's book about violin teaching. At the time, Mozart wrote a brief Kyrie for a four-part chorus and orchestra, based off an French melody. It showed his ability to take in music and create his own version.

They quit Paris on the 9th of July. They headed south, first to Lyon and Dijon before heading to newly independent Geneva that was turbulent. Then they headed to Lausanne where they stayed for a few weeks at the request by King Ludwig from Wurttemberg. After that, they traveled to Berne and Zurich where the orchestral concert was held, which ran from October 1766 to.

The group continued on their Swiss journey and entered German territories, and stopped at Donaueschingen which was where they presented nine concerts over the course of 12 days, much to the satisfaction of the locals. He also performed on the organ along with the young violinist (two years younger than him) Sixtus Bachmann and was named the winner.

Then they made their journey to Munich on the 8th of November when they performed in front of The Elector of Bavaria. They presented the elector Mozart with a melody he had written in pencil that Mozart transformed into a complete composition. However, despite his accomplishments there, Wolfgang got sick, and the two were forced to stay longer than they'd anticipated. At the end of November however they had returned to Salzburg after having been away for more than four years. It was considered a success since they had become famous all over Europe however, Leopold's principal ambition was not fulfilled. Leopold wanted to secure an ongoing place for his son in any of the court in Europe however he not succeeded in this endeavor. So, he began making plans for a second tour next year.

IV

SUCCESSFUL SETBACKS AND SUCCESS VIENNA

"I am one of the people who'll keep doing until all the doings come to the end of their rope."

WOLFGANG AMADEUS MOZART

As soon as Mozart had arrived in Salzburg however, Mozart was asked to compose an essay for the archbishop's ceremony. The work's authorship was challenged by the archbishop who put Mozart in the area for one week, and required him to write an oratorio. The result, KV 35, was highly praised at the time of its debut while the archbishop felt convinced of his talent. To show his recognized talents the archbishop was commissioned to compose a piece specifically for Salzburg's Jesuit academy in Salzburg and it was staged in the spring of 1767. The dramatic work Clementia Croesi is performed along with the Mozart's Apollo et Hyacinthus seu Hyacinthi Metamorphosis.

On the 11th of September, 1767 the Mozart family traveled to Vienna where they stayed with a gold dealer who had three children, all of whom had small pox. Concerned for his children's safety On the 23rd of October, everyone moved out of the city for Brno to avoid the smallpox epidemic which was sweeping the city. On the 26th of October, however after having quit Brno, Mozart began to begin to show signs of the deadly illness, even though they were in Olmutz. Even though Mozart became temporarily blind because from this condition, he was able to recover in November, which was the time Nannerl was diagnosed with the illness. She too was cured and at the close this year they had been all set for a return trip to Vienna. The irony is that it was possible to get an available inoculation against smallpox, however Leopold did not decide to inoculate his children thinking that it could cause harm to their imaginations.

The family left to Vienna in the month of December 1767. visiting Brno over two months on the request of the brother of archbishop of Salzburg and arrived in Vienna on the 10th of January 1768. They were then presented to the Empress Maria Theresa on January 19th and she was delighted to see them.

In the month of January 1768 Leopold Mozart took an informal remark to be a source of inspiration to compose an opera. He was disappointed when his initial opera La Finta Semplice (KV 51) was not performed. The circumstances in Vienna were competitive, however and a series of bizarre intrigues by jealous composers led to the fact that the work wasn't performed in Vienna. Instead, his short musical theatre piece, called one of the most famous opera buffas in French Bastien et

Bastienne, composed during his time in France and performed to high acclaim.

Furthermore, Mozart was asked to compose a Mass, which led to the composition of his Mass of G major (KV 49) which was regarded by some theorists to be the first work of his maturity.

V
THE SOLO TRIP TO ITALY

"Neither an incredibly high level of imagination or intelligence, or both contribute to create genius. Love is love, love, love that's the essence that makes genius."

WOLFGANG AMADEUS MOZART

Preparations

L

eopold believed that to be a true musician, one must travel to Italy to learn. It was a long-standing tradition of German areas, from Hans Leo Hassler, Heinrich Schuetz and Handel that one had to master the music that was the style of Italians.

The date was September 30th, 1769, Leopold received a letter of recommendation from Johann Adolf Hasse, the director of Italianate German music sent at Abbate Giovanni Maria Ortes in Bologna. It's a very adoring picture of parents and children however, Leopold quickly realized that the performances in Italy were always private events and not as common of Austria or the German countries, which meant that payment would take the form of a little trinket, or a small sum of cash, instead of the admission fee he was used to charging. But he was convinced it was vital to arrange this trip and he decided to go ahead the process. The day before the departure, Wolfgang was appointed Konzertmeister to the archbishop.

First Successes

L
eopold and Wolfgang left for Italy on the 13th of December 1769, and left Anna

Maria and Nannerl at their home. Their first destination was Innsbruck in which they were welcomed by the count Johann Nepomuk Spaur, the brother of the Salzburg Cathedral canon. On 15th of July, Mozart sight-read a concerto and was presented with an act of kindness together with 12 ducats.

The group continued on the 19th, and made a stop in the tiny Italian city of Rovereto and there Mozart was greeted with presents from Italian nobles who greeted Mozart. They performed a concert at the residence that belonged to Baron Giovanni Battista Todeschi which was so packed that they had bouncers in order to get to the organ amid the throng of people who were standing in the room. Leopold considered, with a few proofs that if this was the kind of reception they would receive throughout Italy and beyond, they could have gained a lot of attention at the end of their journey.

It was on through Verona which was where operas where presented every night, except on Mondays was the only day that it was impossible for Mozarts to plan the concert. However, when Wolfgang was able to perform a symphony composed by him and read difficult music, and then performed an aria performed by himself in front of the crowd, the residents of Verona were awestruck. He was able to see an opera titled Ruggiero and a libretto composed by Metastasio (composer not known).

Then he went to Mantua on the 10th of January, 1770. There, it was cold, but pleasant. In Mantua his return, he was loved, and especially by the ladies in the town who were crying as he left. He gave an evening of music on January 16 1770. He also attended the Hasse's Demetrio also.

The two traveled to Cremona The town in which the famous Stradivarius, Guarneri, and Amati violins were constructed. He also attended the performance of the Hasse's (libretto composed by the Metastasio) La Clemenza di Tito that he later put to music by himself.

Milan

T
The group travelled to the huge central region of northern Italy, Milan, where they were sheltered within Italy's Augustine monastic community located in San Marco. It was Count Karl Joseph von Firmian, the governor general, served as their host for the duration of the time. They were able to meet the famous music composer Niccolo Piccinni whose opera Cesare in Egitto was produced in the. He was questioned by the famous sacred music composer Giambattista Sammartini. The composer was very impressed by his skills.

After Mozart had captivated the nobles of Milan and Milan, the Count von Firmian commissioned an opera seria by Mozart to be staged by the Teatro Regio Ducal in Milan.

After a string of performances which he received a warm welcome and was well-loved, they returned to Bologna in Italy, in which Padre Martini and the legendary Carlo Broschi, known as Farinelli was retired, entertained musicians in his villa. Farinelli had achieved huge career that was a huge success across Europe with his performances, which included Vienna, Spain, and London and Mozart was extremely impressed by his voice even in older years.

Florence

O
On the 30th of March 1770 when they arrived in Florence where was located the capital of Tuscany and, thanks to letters of recommendations from Austrian nobles and nobles, they were warmly welcomed from their host, the Grand Duke Leopold and the Imperial ambassador and

ambassador, The Count Rosenburg. Mozart got the chance to perform in the court on April 2 with the legendary musician Pietro Nardini, who also provided him with difficult fugues to play. The music director of Florence was Marquis de Ligneville, and the Marquis de Ligneville also placed Mozart through the paces by giving him complex fugues for him to play, which he performed with ease. Additionally, in Milan He came across the famous singer Giovanni Manzuoli who had been acquaintances with the pair in England and discovered that he was approached by Milanese authorities to sing in Mozart's opera. He also had a meeting with Thomas Linley, who was another child prodigy who was a thirteen year old violinist. Linley and Mozart became friends and Linley was afflicted with the tragic fate of dying young when he was drowned in boating accident in 1778.

Rome

A

Though they wanted to stay in Florence however, they were aware that they needed to get to Rome in time for Holy Week to gain maximum recognition, therefore, they left in a miserable weather, where the hotels were hostile and filthy, as well as roads were inaccessible. But they made it to Rome on April 11 with thunderclaps so loud that caused them to believe Rome was under siege.

The Mozarts arrived just in time to listen to their rendition of the Allegri Miserere, a piece important for members of the Sistine Chapel choir, performed only on Friday and Wednesday in Holy Week, written for two choirs. One of four parts and the other with five parts, that are joined at the final section of the work with nine harmony parts. Mozart was able to hear it twice, before returning back to his house to record the notes exactly from his memory, making the first official copy of this highly guarded possession of the

Vatican. It is crucial to realize that this is a nine-part medley that runs for around twenty minutes. There are many repetitions in the work, since it is composed in a manner similar to an octave (with the section being repeated following a different section, which is repeated every few minutes) This feat is both amazing and typical of young Mozart. He was 14 years old at the time he performed this feat however, it was not his intention, he was unaware of the significance of this piece, the piece was taught to him about its importance and importance of keeping it secret. However, he was able to recreate the piece despite the warning that it should not be distributed to those who weren't in the Sistine Chapel.

Chapter 8: More Journeys To Italy

The pair they left Rome in May on the 8th. They headed south towards Naples the other city in famous Italian opera. The pair arrived at Naples on May 14th.

With the letters of recommendation, they Mozarts were soon performing the concert on May 28, and also attended the debut show of Niccolo Jommelli's opera Armida abbandonata at the famed San Carlo theatre. Mozart was asked to compose one of his operas for the coming season at San Carlo, but he did not accept due to his prior engagement to Milan. Unfortunately, they weren't invited to perform at the royal court, and Leopold chose to quit Naples and go back to Rome after a visit to the popular tourist attractions in Mount Vesuvius, the twin towns that are buried, Herculaneum and Pompeii and the Roman baths in Baiae. They set off for Rome on June 25.

At Rome, Mozart was granted an audience with the Pope and was appointed an honorary knight in the Order of the Golden Spur. Mozart and his companions left Rome and headed back to Bologna to arrive on the 20th of July. While in Bologna, Mozart got a libretto (significantly but not the one they were expecting Metastasio's La Nitteti, but Mitridate, Re di Ponto composed created by Vittorio Cigna-Santi) following Giuseppe Parini's Italian adaptation of Jean Racine's work, Mithridate.

Based on a thorough analysis of La Nitteti by Josef Myslivecek who was a friend of his in Milan The opera was created and crafted to be staged in Bologna at the time that Mozart was introduced to Myslivecek and the opera was mostly composed while the two were in Bologna and with (one supposes) some assistance from Myslivecek. Mozart was able to learn a lot about composition for opera from his mentor and used some of his musical themes to compose his own.

When he composed this piece, Mozart applied for membership to the Accademia Filarmonica in Bologna. On the 9th of October, 1770 Mozart was a candidate for the examination to be admitted to the. Mozart was required to compose the four-part work for voices and, despite being given four hours to complete his creation, Mozart finished it in one hour, and was appointed to the Accademia in spite of the requirement to be 20 years old.

On October 18th they came back to Milan on the 18th of October when he had finished writing and creating the Mitradate operas. This was a task he was required to write in extensive discussion with the singers, who held a lot of control over the songs they sang.

The opera premiered on the Teatro Regio Ducal in Milan on December 26, 1770 (at the Milan Carnival) and under the direction of Mozart. It was a huge success and was performed 21 times, despite doubts arising from Mozart's young age, which was only 14 when he wrote the opera. Unfortunately, for the sake of musical history the opera was not revived until the 20th century, because the original score is lost (but certain manuscripts are being rediscovered). The opera is a masterpiece of singing arias of the principal roles, however there are only two short ensembles, which was common that was popular at the time. A single suet is heard at the beginning of Act II, and the quintet's finale.

The result led to more opera orders from Milan In the month of October in 1771, his work received given the task of writing Ascanio at Alba in 1771, and Lucio Silla in 1772.

For the rest of his travels, Mozart visited Venice and was well-liked by the aristocratic residents of the city. He attended many operas, and performed at numerous private functions, as being a part of the Carnevale that made Venice was renowned. They set off towards Salzburg and arrived on March 28 and were given a new contract for an opera set in Milan to premiere in the carnival of 1773. (this opera was Lucio Silla as well as the other operawas Ascanio in Alba that began as a serenata but morphed into an opera, and was presented at Milan at the end of 1771).

Leopold as well as Wolfgang Leopold and Wolfgang returned to Salzburg in December 1771 following the fact that Mozart had completed his Symphony (KV 112) at the end of December, and afterward, he became very in a serious illness. While they were absent the Archbishop Siegmund Schrattenbach had died on December 16th following a long illness while his successor who was the previous bishop from Gurk did not seem to be a well-liked selection. Mozart got the job to compose an opera to mark the entrance to the city of the archbishop's new appointment that would take place in 1772. Mozart composed a serenata Il sogno of Scipione (KV 266)) to a text written by Metastasio (adapted to accommodate the circumstances in Salzburg).

In 1772 Mozart was in Salzburg and composed an Symphony (KV 128, 129, 130) in February and three more in the month of May (KV 128, 130, 129). In August and July Mozart composed three more orchestras, (KV 132 (133, 132, as well as 134). The Archbishop of the time appointed Mozart as Konzertmeister permanent with 150 florins per year which assisted a good lot in his financial position.

On the 24th of October The two male Mozarts took off for Milan arriving on the 4th of November, and started to get acquainted and sing with singers. The premiere took place on the 26th of December and was a great success despite some oddities and Mozart was satisfied with the outcome. In January 1773, as he was waiting to know whether Wolfgang was appointed to a post in the music industry at the prestigious Italian school of Tuscany, Mozart wrote a sequence that he called "Milanese" strings quartets (KV 160/159a, 155/134a, and 160/159a) and his solo motet Exsultate and jubilate KV 165, which was composed for the main character of his opera Rauzzini. It is a stunning sacred work, which is played regularly.

Unfortunately, the appointment to Florence was never made the appointment was never made, and Leopold only became aware about it the following day, February 27th which led Leopold to justify his lengthy absence from Salzburg with the claim that the severity of his rheumatism hindered him from traveling. They left Milan in March on the fourth of March, and arrived in Salzburg nine days later with no Italian appointment and suffering from depression due to this. Mozart did not return to Italy following this.

VI

SALZBURG TO VIENNA

"I cannot write poetry since I am not a poet. I'm not able to craft beautiful artistic phrases that create shadow and light because I am not a painter. I am unable to through signs or pantomimes express my thoughts and feelings because I'm not a dancer, but I can with tones because I am a musician."

WOLFGANG AMADEUS MOZART

After his return from Italy on the 13th of March 1773 Mozart went back to duties at the court of Archbishop of the Prince Hieronymus Colloredo. Mozart took advantage of this to compose a variety of diverse works, including brand new symphonies and piano works, and violin sonatas. He also wrote strings quartets, masses serenades, masses, and some less important operas. Between March and December 1775, Mozart began writing violin concertos, and later wrote five. They were his only concertos for violin that he ever composed. The three concertos he wrote, KV 218, KV 218 and KV 219 are often played.

The composer was born in 1776 and started writing piano concertos. They culminated at the end of the concerto in E flat, KV 271 in 1777. It was deemed by critics as an absolute masterpiece in the genre, and a mature piece.

It is difficult to consider these musical innovations without context they are incredibly important, and Mozart was not content in Salzburg. He had been exposed to the most outstanding works of famous Italian composers and believed that Salzburg in spite of its potential it was an insignificant place. He continued to seek jobs in other, more prestigious centers. Mozart would like create more operas and there were few opportunities to write operas in Salzburg. Then the court theatre was closed in 1775, which made these opportunities more scarce.

To secure a job, Mozart recognized that Vienna was the most likely place to go He and his father left on July 14th, 1773 to Austria's capital, Vienna. Austrian Empire. He remained until September 1773.

Doing their best to get an unassailable position, Mozart and his father realized that they were at a stumbling block in his growth. He was 17 years old and was far too old to be considered a child prodigy and also far too inexperienced to be considered to be a serious contender in the adult world. He did manage to score an opportunity to meet the Empress Maria Theresa on August 4th however nothing was to be gained from it, despite her generosity to him. In an effort to find work He made friends with one of the violinists, Franz Griebich, of the Imperial string quartet, which frequently performed at the court. Mozart composed six string quartets (KV 168-172) and was influenced through the works of well-known composer Franz Joseph Haydn. They are the very first four quartets Mozart composed with four movements. A number of them contained fugues (KV 173 and 168) in the last movement. The first section in KV 170, instead of being in the sonata-allegro format, is actually an arrangement of variations on a subject. He also composed a set of variations that derived from Antonio Salieri's aria for the court composer in La hota di Venezia that was recently a hit in Vienna.

The time in Vienna was a complete failure for a young composer often adolescent. The two quit Vienna on the 24th of September, and returned just a few days later. He was the Prince of Archbishop who was sick for a good portion of the summer (curtailing music events due to it) was able to recover by September but he passed away on January 1st of the following year, 1774.

After their return in Salzburg, Mozart completed two Symphony in a short time: KV 182, which is well-written, but not a masterpiece and was completed on the

3rd of October in addition to KV 183, the "little" G minor Symphony, KV 183, completed on October 5, which is considered to be a masterpiece. The reason for the significance of this work is the most recent artistic and musical advancement that is known by the name of Sturm und Drang (literally "storm and stress") that became the basis for the Romantic style in the later century. Sturm und Drang is a style that is largely connected to that of Haydn during this period and it is thought that Mozart was awed of the most charming and friendly of composers but there isn't any historical evidence to suggest that he actually had a conversation with Haydn when he visited Vienna.

While in Salzburg He was a friend by Joseph Haydn's famous musician brother Michael Haydn, who was working for the courts. He was aided and inspired by the kind man and was encouraged to compose sacred music. He composed two masses, one in F (KV 1924) and the second in D (KV 194).

Haydn was heavily influenced through the Viennese style of Michael Haydn's older brother but also by the famous Mannheim school, which produced amazing early classical symphonies composed by Stamitz and Graun. The reason Mozart composed numerous symphonies during the time isn't clear but it is certain that his work stood him well in the decades to come.

While his time in Salzburg was a bit tame in comparison to his previous successes in Italy However, he received an order from Munich to compose his carnival-themed opera in 1775. He travelled to Munich from the 6th of December 1774, until March 1775 but his only achievement was the successful staging of his work La finta giardiniera. Just after arriving the toothache began to develop which forced him to delay the opening from December 29th until January 5th. Unfortunately, due to issues in the singing group, the premiere was delayed further and was finally opened on the 13th of January. In a strange twist, Antonio Tozzi, who had been the star of the show last year thanks to his impressive operetta buffa performance, got given the task to compose the opera seria that was surpassed by Mozart's La finta giardiniera. Mozart was especially happy as the sister of his Nannerl was in attendance to watch his accomplishment.

After returning to Salzburg after a highly great run of his production but with no permanent position that him and his father were hoping for, he left empty handed. Then he started something novel and would cement his name in the future years and that was writing piano solo sonatas. The first collection of piano sonatas, KV 279-284 are dedicated to the Baron von Durnitz, an amateur keyboardist and bassoonist who was unable to pay Mozart for the work. They were nevertheless staples of Mozart's subsequent concerts throughout Mannheim in Mannheim and Paris.

In the same way Many the keyboard concerts he composed such as the three-keyboard-concerto (KV 242) were composed for his students, which were typically women who were part of the noble class from Salzburg and the areas around.

VII

AUGSBURG, MANNHEIM, PARIS and MUNICH

"We are here in order to continue to grow tirelessly and to inspire one another through debate and to do our best to encourage the advancement of art and science."

WOLFGANG AMADEUS MOZART

In 1777, in August, Mozart requested another leave of absence from Archbishop Colloredo however, he was turned down. The Archbishop was so upset by his refusal that he was able to dismiss the two of

them, Wolfgang as well as Leopold. He wrote:
"Father and son have been granted permission to search for their fortune elsewhere according to Jesus' Gospel."
It was a fact that placed them both in a tough financial situation however on September 23, Mozart set out in the search of a permanent job going to Munich, Augsburg, Mannheim as well as Paris.

Instead of joining the father who was required to argue for his place in court and again, his father decided Wolfgang would be going to court with his mom. This was an ideal idea, but it did not go as planned.

The first visit was Munich in which he had achieved great success just a few years prior. Although he had every letter of reference he could locate as well as his knighthood award from the Pope and an offer to write four operas for the next year's season, the elector determined that they wanted Mozart to "go to Italy," suggesting that Mozart was unaware of his early popularity in Italy. Thus, there were very only a few possibilities for employment in Italy. The main event that he remembers was when he first encountered the concept of an German opera. After that, he was convinced that opera was appropriate to the German language and wanted to compose one in German should he be able to secure the opportunity to write a piece.

In Augsburg the aforementioned Augsburg, he got acquainted with his cousin from a distant family, Maria Anna Thekla who he called "Basle." They evidently bonded and may have become lovers, as the letters he wrote to her suggest:
"I love your hand or your face, knees, and even your with a single word: everything I let you kiss!"
This bizarre moment hints at the gradual adulthood Mozart enjoyed so much, and that his father was so afraid of.

There weren't any opportunities available for him in Munich or Augsburg however, he had established some contacts while during his time in Salzburg as well as Vienna with some of the most renowned orchestra in Europe The Mannheim orchestra. A lot people from them convinced him that he could be successful in Mannheim.

Mannheim

W
When he was while in Mannheim during the autumn of 1777, Mozart discovered and was in love with the beautiful AloysiaWeber, an actress from a musical lineage who was a resident of Vienna and Mannheim and was the sibling of the legendary German writer Carl Maria Von Weber's father Franz.

Johann Baptist Wendling, the principal flutist of the Mannheim orchestra He introduced Mozart to an amateur flutist with a wealth of experience named

Ferdinand De Jean, who was a surgeon with the Dutch East India Company. Mozart frequently adapted his compositions for the particular musical or social context His parents insisted that his son take any commission, no matter whether they were small or not well-paid. De Jean commissioned Mozart to compose three simple flute concertos as well as two flute quartets. Even though the flute was a subject of controversy for him, he however, he agreed to accept. Mozart seemed to was a complete snob and this hatred only grew more pronounced when the amateur was forced to pay Mozart just half of the amount that he promised him. However, Mozart completed a D-major quartet on the 25th of December 1777. He composed the piece as per De Jean's instructions and in the style of the string quartet.

Following this disappointing experience, Mozart realized that there was a lack of opportunities for employment in Mannheim however he decided to set on with his wife to Paris on the 14th of March 1778.

When Mozart lived living in Paris, Aloysia was hired as an actress in Munich during the time and her entire family relocated to Munich. When Mozart was passing through Munich as he returned home, she resented his presence, however he continued to stay in contact with his family even after the family moved to Vienna. He later married the younger daughter of her, Constanze, when he moved into a house at the home of the family in the home of the Webers in Vienna.

Paris

I

In Paris, Mozart found life quite comfortable initially when he stayed with the Ambassador Grimm. But after a few months they fell out as Mozart as well as his mom were made to live in a shady hotel. Mozart began to sink into debt, and began to pawn his wealth. It was a fact that Mozart did not speak fluent French and didn't have the drive that his father did. His mother, scared of traveling to foreign countries, was shivering in the cold, unheated space and Wolfgang was out trying get to know Marie Antoinette, the daughter of Maria Theresa, and wife of Louis XVI.

Due to the uncomfortable living conditions her health started to decline, and when Mozart refused to receive treatment by French doctors, her condition was deemed to be dangerous. On the 3rd of July, 1778 Mozart composed a letter of a state of great sorrow:
"I have extremely sad and painful news to share with you that, in actuality, is the reason I haven't responded earlier to your message. My beloved mother is sick. She has been bled in accordance with the customs that was needed and did her lots of good. However, a few days later she began complaining of shivering and high fever. As she deteriorated each minute, she could barely speak and had lost the

ability to hear, she were forced to shout at her. Baron Grimm (the Bavarian ambassador in the hotel where was in his residence] sent his doctor to examine her. She's still extremely fragile, still feverish and delusional. It gives me a little hope, but I do not have much. I was adrift between hope and anxiety night and day however, I'm now completely resigned to God's will. God and pray that you as well as my sibling are too... Let's put aside these negative thoughts and continue to believe however, only a little... I've composed a symphony to mark the beginning to the "Concert Spirituel" that was performed to arousing praise during Corpus Christi day. I was extremely nervous during the rehearsal , because throughout my entire life I've never witnessed something go as badly. It's impossible to make sense of how they ran around and scratched it two times. I was very nervous and would have liked to see it repeated but it was not possible. Then, I went to bed with a heavy heart, angry and disappointed. The next morning, I decided to not attend the concert however, the pleasant night weather forced me to change my decision. I was determined that, if the performance ended as bad as the rehearsal I would enter the orchestra, pick up the violin of the first violinist, and then lead the orchestra myself."

It was not known to him at the time of composition, Anna Maria Mozart would pass away that evening. This was his "Paris" Symphony in D major (KV 297) composed by Mozart to accompany the Concert Spirituel. The world premiere was held on the 12th of June 1778 in private performances at the residence of the Count of Karl Heinrich Joseph von Sickingen who was Ambassador to the Electorate of the Palatinate. The public premiere took place for six days later, on June 26th 1778 in the Concert Spirituel and then on the 15th of August.

In spite of immense sadness and sorrow due to the disease that would eventually cause the death of his mother, Mozart wrote an impressive Symphony. It's scored to two flutes, two Oboes two clarinets of A 2 and 2 bassoons, two French trumpets, two horns with timpani, strings (twenty-two violins five violas and eight 'cellos and five basses). It is also the first Mozart Symphony to employ clarinets.

It's also composed of three movements, with the exception of the minuet and the trio (third) movement. Furthermore, the first starts with a rising theme that is characteristic for this particular Mannheim school. The effect, when combined with a large crescendo is known as Mannheim Rocket. Mannheim Rocket. The letter he sent to his dad after he had slammed his audience and orchestra:
"In in the middle of opening Allegro the composer wrote a section I was sure people would enjoy and the entire audience was completely captivated by it and there was huge applause. However, I was aware when I composed it what kind of effect it would have, that's why I

brought it back in the final minutes which resulted in it was re-aired."

It is evident that Mozart has learned how to wow an audience. He did, however many other circumstances also stopped him from accepting a position in France. He was contemplating at one moment that he might have been offered a position as organist at Versailles that would have required only a few months and earned him a salary of 2 000 livres However, he also stated that he would never taken the offer. For the sake of history, that's an excellent thing considering how the family of royals will develop in France.

Sonata-Allegro Form

M
Ozart was the master of this style, the most malleable of forms and also the most Classical form. It evolved from various forms that were popular in the time. Mozart was a natural fan of the Mannheim school of composition and playing often stating his desire to be a part of it. It was

the place that was founded by Johann Stamitz, Jiri Antonin Benda along with Franz Xaver Richter, where the famous orchestra, whose stunning style is commonly called"the Mannheim Rocket (or Steamroller) composed their symphonies which have been so influential to the style he was developing.

Mozart was a sponge that absorbed these influences as sponges and proceeded to develop what is thought to be the most sophisticated of music forms of the Classical repertoire. Unfortunately, his music might be evolving in the eyes of the contemporary listener however, not as much as the other Viennese composers who were around his, which is the reason Mozart was unable to secure an appointment at the court (that as well as the fact that his conduct was not the most exemplary and could even be rude to the people in his vicinity!).

However, his method of communication was the sonata form , the flexible and beautiful representation of the philosophy of the Enlightenment and akin to the modern legal system (Common Law, and, a bit later in time, Code Napoleon). Code Napoleon), where rivals compete for supremacy, or through science (where theories are presented, tested and then and tested and, on result concluding) or, in the case of the brilliant Hegelian dialectic (in the course of which two conflicting discourse topics are presented to be discussed, debated and finally solved). Sonatas typically contain a variety of topics (musical melody, chord progressions and important areas, or other elements that are easily recognized) that are then described (in"Exposition"), which is followed by "Exposition") and is repeated twice to emphasize and then discussed (in"Development"), then discussed "Development" in which they are tossed around in different keys, arranged and testable) Then, they are resolved (in"Recapitulation") "Recapitulation"). This particular system, perfect in sync with the Enlightenment is perhaps somewhat out of date, due to the autocratic rule of the city and the involvement of the exact people he sought to patronize as!

Paris Again

W
While Mozart was while Mozart was in Paris, Leopold had been trying to secure Mozart his post back in the form of telling his Archbishop about his accomplishments, therefore, the Archbishop agreed to restore Wolfgang to his post as a Konzertmeister, with a pay that was five hundred dollars. Leopold addressed a letter Wolfgang to inform him of the good news and also to inform him that the gorgeous young woman Aloysia Weber, with whom the singer had fallen in love with, was not just to perform on stage in Salzburg but was also going to live in the house of Leopold. The news was enough to make it easier for Mozart of his desire to go

back to Salzburg. In the autumn of 1778, Mozart embarked on a journey to Salzburg with a stop first at Strasbourg where he performed a few concertsbefore moving to Mannheim. Mannheim was always loved by Mozart and according to his own words "the way I enjoy Mannheim, Mannheim loves me as well," he wrote his father. The only person to not like Mannheim Mannheim It seems that it was the actress Aloysia Weber. She was the first person he saw there, was able to make it clear that his affection to her wasn't shared. He wrote a duodrama titled Semiramis which was in the style of the legendary Mannheim composer Benda that has unfortunately gone undiscovered.

Mozart was in Salzburg in the beginning of January 1779. In his time in Salzburg Mozart wrote the mass that is an outstanding work, but is not widely recognized. There is also a possibility that he wrote an opera titled Zaide that is almost gone today.

In the autumn of 1780 Mozart had a conversation with a friend who could become an important collaborator. Emanuel Schikaneder had a German theatre troupe that was based in Vienna however, they also was in Salzburg in 1780. Schikaneder became a friend of the family of the Mozarts and the Mozarts were frequent visitors to his performances. Then, Schikaneder would become the librettist of Mozart's brilliant German Singspiel (play with songs or, as we call it now be able to call musical), The Magic Flute.

VIII

MUNICH AND IDOMENEO

"I am grateful to my God for granting me the chance to learn about death as the key that will open the door to absolute happiness."

WOLFGANG AMADEUS MOZART

In 1780, Mozart received his first official order from Munich for an opera seria based on the theme of the King of Crete: Idomeneo. After three days of transit, Mozart arrived in Munich in the month of November 1779. Here, the composer was provided with perfect working conditions. He then wrote what is believed to be the first mature work. He was blessed with the amazing Mannheim orchestra to collaborate with, as well as the world-class group of singers employed by the by the elector of Pfalz, Karl Theodor, available to him. He had collaborated successfully with the director of the theater, Joseph Count Seeau in Munich for his production La Finta Giardiniera. The libretto was inspired by the play Idomenee written by Antoine Danchet but was reworked into Italian by the

Salzburg court chaplain Giambattista Varesco.

Since Mozart enjoyed greater recognition than Varesco and Varesco, he had the ability to exert enormous influence on the libretto. The composer was eager to challenge some of the traditional operatic conventions to create something totally original and captivating.

Idomeneo is a poetic drama with the shape in an opera-seria, with several new, effective characteristics including the increase in instrumentation of the orchestra, and the increased usage of choruses. It is widely regarded as the most choral of Mozart's operas. The composer also had an influence on the dramaturgy. He also shortened sections to enhance their effect and increased suspense through the instrumentation and composed the amazing ballet music. The premiere of the ballet in Munich during 1781, at the Residenz Theatre was a great success. Indeed, it was so ecstatic was Mozart after the performance that he stayed there for three months and took in Carnival season in fullest. It was only when the Archbishop from Salzburg invited Mozart returning to Salzburg to end the most pleasurable time in his entire life Mozart went to Munich.

IX
MOZART IN VIENNA

"How sad to see these wonderful gentlemen accept what they are told and not make their own decisions! It's never the case."

WOLFGANG AMADEUS MOZART

It is believed that the Archbishop of Salzburg is believed to be determined to bring Mozart's self-confidence to a level that was manageable. He were summoned into Vienna in the summer of 1898, where the court had changed to a new location, and his pay was cut to 400 florins and his place at the table was reduced to a table with cooks and the other servants with menial jobs. When Mozart requested permission to perform an appearance in Vienna however, the Archbishop denied the request. in addition, when he requested to be allowed to attend a concert alongside the Countess Thun in order to have an audience with the Emperor Joseph II, he was denied. In the end, Mozart left, reneging on his income and residence and sought a home to stay within Vienna along with members of the Weber family. They began taking boarders in from the time Fridolin the father passed away. To supplement the small amount of money that he earned from commissions Mozart began giving piano lessons.

Leopold was adamant that to maintain his position within the Salzburg court Salzburg in the Salzburg court, he should side with the Archbishop in this dispute and, as a result, Mozart temporarily lost touch with his father. It was surely an affront to him, considering that Mozart had just lost his mother, too.

Mozart got introduced to magnificent keyboard works by Johann Sebastian Bach, and especially the forty-eight preludes as well as fugues referred to as The Well-Tempered Clavier thanks to the generous arts patron, Baron Gottfried Von Swieten (1733-1803).

Mozart was always seeking work and commissions as well as permanent appointments from nobles However, nothing could be found. He began working on his escape operetta, The Abduction from the Seraglio in 1781 in the month of September, however, due to numerous obstacles during its creation the composer gave up on the opera for the moment.

Constanze Weber

While things weren't getting better for professional Mozart He had started to pursue Constanze Weber The older daughter of his previous lover, Aloysia Weber, who is now at Vienna together with her entire family. When Leopold discovered this love story the couple had a conversation, and he wrote to Wolfgang to ask him to put things to rest because he believed it would harm his career. Mozart replied to assure his father that there was nothing happening, and even left Weber's home to dispel the gossip. However, in December, he wrote to his father, asking his approval for the marriage which his father reluctantly agreed to but his father had was not a believer in the union and fought it as a snub against Wolfgang until his death in 1787. But, things moved quickly for the lovers and on August 4 they got married just a few days after his first success in performance of the opera Vienna. Mozart as well as Constanze were happily married and had six children in the same household which included two who lived into adulthood. The burden of poverty began to plague them during the last years of their marriage but happiness was also able to be a constant companion. Rarely in the history of music has a couple been so happy. Both shared the love for and musical talent, and Constanze was a loyal and fun-loving wife of the fun-loving Mozart. While they were in Salzburg in the following year, she performed the solo of a soprano in Mozart's Mass of C Minor KV 427.

the Abduction from the Seraglio

M
Ozart's debut great German operetta, The Abduction from the Seraglio it premiered on the 16th of July 1782. It was also performed at in the Vienna Burgtheater.

Joseph II had devised an initiative dubbed the Nationalsingspiel which was also known as the National singing theater, to combat the trend of Italian opera that had an uncontrollable grip on this fundamentally German-speaking city. Mozart's operetta was the initial production of the new organization led by Gottfried Stephanie, who later became the librettist. Actually, the opera was, besides several important translations of Italian operettas, the sole profitable project from this endeavor, which was eventually abandoned because of its failing.

Mozart wrote the opera quick, believing that it would take him only two months to complete the whole opera. But, he received an extension when they substituted for a Gluck opera for the event it was originally planned for the opera to be performed in the following summer. His father persuaded him to write in the form his thoughts about the significance of the composer and the librettist (writer of the text). In a letter that he wrote to his father, dated 13th October 1781 the writer wrote that

"I think"in an opera the poet must be an unwavering child of the music. What is the reason why Italian comic operas so well-known across the globe despite their terrible librettos? The reason is that music is the king and, as you listen, everything else gets lost. Opera is a certain success when the story is clearly planned and the lyrics are written solely for the music and are not forced in one or the other to fit the savage rhyme. The best part is when a skilled composer, who knows the theater and has the ability to be able to make sound judgements meet a skilled poet, a real phoenix. When this happens, there is no need to worry about applause, not even from those who don't know."

Mozart's views on the role of the librettist are important because, ever since its inception at the time of 1600, opera lent importance for the libretto. The librettists who wrote the texts were usually noblemen, while often the composers were seen as servants to noblemen even great composers such as Monteverdi or Cavalli were treated with a snide manner as their music was replaced by the music of a different composer, and the words were considered sacred territory. The librettists sold their poems at operas however composers were often not even acknowledged at all. It took someone who was famous and had the talent of Mozart to affirm the importance of music and to alter this unjust importance of the libretto at the expense of the music.

For a long time, Mozart had written a style of music that has been largely ignored known as the divertimento. He was able to get an appointment in the court of Emperors, however it wasn't the prestigious post he had always hoped to get. He was instead responsible for creating music for the garden of the royal court and set to writing these lengthy and frequently repetitive pieces however, they were a bit of genius, too. In the first year he was on his own as a result of this job He composed two serenades as well as an oboe divertimento Another serenade for two clarinets, two oboes and two bassoons. He also composed a symphony, in D as well as two concertos. The composer was less prolific the year he was forced to instruct students in music every day to earn a living. The life of a free musician is often thought of as a liberating experience and romanticized by writers who didn't suffer from privilege, but each of Mozart as well as Beethoven were constantly looking for patrons despite the obvious fact that patronage's golden age was quickly coming to an end.

Mozart and Haydn

It was in 1784 that Mozart had a chance to meet Joseph Haydn the famous symphonist and aspiring composer for opera and soon began to become friends. Even though Haydn was in the midst of his work for most of the time in Esterhaza, the country estate of a wealthy Hungarian nobleman and was at Vienna it was possible for him to search Mozart out and they would both perform their respective string quartets. Haydn's opus 20 string quartets composed in 1772, which he called"the "Sun Quartets" were generally regarded as the source of inspiration for Mozart's 1773 KV168-173 quartets he composed in Vienna. They likely first came in person during a concert where both of their works were being played, on the 22nd and 23rd 1783. Haydn was 52 and the most well-known composer in Europe in the time. Mozart was just a teenager with a stage play The Abduction from the Seraglio was premiered with great success at Vienna and was currently being performed in a variety of European cities.

The factor which brought them closer was their shared passion for the string quartet and the string quartet, which they both composed. They also composed an ensemble with Haydn played the violin, the legendary operetta composer Carl Ditters von Dittersdorf played the second violin, Mozart played viola, and composer Vanhal played the 'cello. Mozart committed the six quartets he composed (Mozart's "Haydn" quartets (KV 387, KV 421, 428 and KV 458 KV 464 and 465) which were published in 1785 and dedicated to Haydn as a reaction the Haydn's Opus 33 from 1781. The dedication of the work to another composer was unusual in the time, and so was the dedication he affixed his work to:

"A father who chosen to send his sons into the world, saw it was his duty to leave them under the safety and direction of a man who was a celebrity in the day and also, in the most important sense to become his greatest friend. Similar to that I am sending my six sons to your care. [...] So, please accept them with kindness and serve as an example of a father, guide and best friend! [...] I ask you to accept the flaws that might have been snubbed by a father's eyes and, despite these, continue to maintain your warm and loving friendship with someone who is so grateful for it."

Even though at this point, Mozart was very successful and was comfortable in high-end locations, and sending his children into expensive schools for private education, he also had many critics. It is worthwhile to mention that Haydn behaved with respect and as kind of a mentor for Mozart as he helped him with his professional life. He once stated about Mozart: "If only I could imitate Mozart's incredible abilities to touch the souls of every musician and on the souls and nobles' souls particularly by expressing them as profoundly and with the same understanding and profundity, as I feel and understand these things, all nations could compete with one another to have such a precious gem." Mozart, for his part, was loved by Haydn and was incredibly impressed by his ability.

Freelance Musician

F
From 1782 until 1785 Mozart was the first to begin a project that would become an essential element for musicians who were independent performing with himself as soloists performing three or four new piano concertos every season. The first time he performed such a concert Mozart composed the B-flat piano concerto,

and finished it just two days prior to the concert. Because theaters were very limited in Vienna He often reserved venues that were unusual: one occasion, he staged the concert in a big space in an apartment known as the Trattnerhof as well as at another point, he rented the ballroom at the Mehlgrube (a restaurant). These performances became extremely popular and the concertos they premiered remain a part of the repertoire.

The musician earned a lot of money from these performances, in turn, Mozart as well as his spouse started to lead a lavish life. They relocated from their modest house to a luxurious apartment that had a rent of 460 florins annually. Mozart also purchased a costly fortepiano (an earlier version of a pianoforte which had a particularly tough action and pedals controlled by your knees) from Anton Walter for nine hundred florins. He also purchased a gorgeous Billiard table for 300 florins. Mozart also bought a billiard table for about three hundred florins. Mozarts took their child Karl Thomas to an exclusive school for boarding and also employed several servants. As was typical of the life of Mozart, the composer never thought to saving money. this short period of financial security made his years of plight, his last years, more difficult to bear. He lived in a luxurious home located on Schulerstrasse close to St Stephen's Cathedral for 460 dollars a year. This was higher than the annual income as an archbishops of Salzburg.

Mozart's Children

Mozart and Constanze Weber welcomed the first of their children,

Raimund Leopold on June 17th, 1783. But by the 19th of August the day he died. In spite of this tragic loss to their family they had five more youngsters: Karl Thomas, who was born on the 21st of September 1784 (who had a long and successful life with many fascinating professions, but none was in the field of music till the year 1858), Johann Thomas Leopold who was born on the 18th, 1786. He passed away on the 15th of November the same year. Their first daughter was Theresia Constanzia Adelheid Friedericke Anna, was born at birth on December 27 1787, was alive until June 29th in 1788 as well as Anna Maria, who was born on the 16th of November 1789, however, she passed away on the same day.

A son younger to Wolfgang and Constanze was Franz Xaver Wolfgang who was born on the 26th of July 1791. He made an enviable career of traveling across Europe as well as playing his father's songs, promoting him by the name of Wolfgang Amadeus Mozart Junior. He was a talented composer with solid credentials and had studied alongside Hummel and Salieri as well as Beethoven. Even though he was able to have a prosperous career as composer, he did not reach the levels of his father, and was never able to escape the impact of the shadows of his father. He passed away in 1844.

It was 1784 when Mozart began keeping an account of his compositions. It also included the date of each composition. Some of these compositions were composed in a rush. For instance, he wrote his Sonata in B-flat, for piano and violin (KV 454) for female violinist Regina Strinasacchi, but only fully notated the violin portion. However, he improvised the piano piece with minimal effort.

Chapter 9: Mature Style 1786-90

"My Constanze is the virtuous and honorable, discrete and loyal lover of her kind and honest Mozart."
WOLFGANG AMADEUS MOZART

Despite the enormous popularity in The Abduction from the Seraglio, Mozart did relatively little operatic writing over the next four years. He wrote only a few unfinished works , including the one-act Singspiel known as Der Schauspieldirektor. He primarily focused on his work as a pianist soloist and composer of concertos. At the end of 1785, Mozart moved away from writing for keyboards and began his famous operatic collaboration composer Lorenzo Da Ponte.

Lorenzo Da Ponte (born Emanuele Conegliano on March 10 1749, died August 17th 1838) was an Italian-born then American opera poet, librettist as well as a Roman Catholic priest. He wrote the libretti to twenty-eight of the operas written by 11 different composers, among them three of Mozart's most acclaimed operas: Don Giovanni (1786), The Marriage of Figaro (1787) and Cosi Fan Tutte (1790).

Born Jewish He was converted into Roman Catholicism with his family in 1864 so that his father could get married to an Jewish woman. Da Ponte was a priest in 1770. was granted minor priestly orders and later became an instructor of literary studies. While being a priest but he appears to have had a rather unconventional life having a lover and having two children with her. The year 1779 was the time he got charged with indecency due to this (and because the brothel was his home and he was brothel, and was arranging entertainments in members of the brothel) and was exiled from Venice for

15 years. Then, in 1781, he relocated to the small town of Austria and later Dresden where he utilized his connections with the nobility to secure an introduction letter from his friend, the Imperial Court Composer, Antonio Salieri. The connection resulted in the appointment of his librettist to his Italian theater in Vienna and also was patronized by Banker Raimund Wetzlar von plankenstern who was also a patron to Mozart.

It is interesting to note that Mozart as well as da Ponte got along very well. Even though his first two operas collaborating with Mozart were conceived to be written by Mozart however, his third opera Cosi fan tutte created by Salieri but was completed by Mozart and da Ponte, which caused animosity in the relationship between both composers.

In 1790, after the Emperor Joseph II passed away, da Ponte lost his patronage and was forced to move to Paris which was in a city where revolutions were taking place. He relocated to London with his lover and four children. He then moved to America in 1790, where he was able to settle in New Jersey as a greengrocer. In the following years, he started the New York Opera Company, which later became known as the Metropolitan Opera Company, and was an citizen of the United States. American citizen.

One of the first collaborative works between Mozart as well as da Ponte took place in The Marriage of Figaro, which was based on one of the three plays written of works by French playwright Beaumarchais named La folle journee or le Mariage de Figaro (The Mad Day also known as The Marriage of Figaro). It was initially intended to be an attack on the French law, known as "the droit de seigneur, under where the Lord of the land was entitled to marry any bride who had permission to wed within his territory. In the preface to the libretto da Ponte wrote:

"I have not created an attempt to translate, but an imitative, let's say , an extract .... I was forced to cut down the original sixteen characters to eleven, which means that two could be performed by a single actor . I also had to eliminate the possibility of a whole act, numerous powerful scenes. .... However, in spite of the determination and effort of the composer and myself to make the opera short the production is not one of the most concise. .... The reason is the wide range of the plot ... for me to portray accurately and in full color all the emotions that are stirred and ... for it to present the audience with a brand new style of spectacle ...."

To be fair, he did deliver on his commitment. The premiere took place in the Burgtheater in Vienna on May 1, 1786. The play tells the story of how employees Figaro and Susanna have a successful wedding in a way that defuse the efforts of their lover's employer, The Count Almaviva to attract Susanna and teach Almaviva the value of loyalty. The reality it was Mozart along with da Ponte came together together effectively together is what resulted in an amazing music drama unlike anything that the world has ever seen before, and that made operas more admired and also caused the opera style, known as opera seria to fade and fade away.

While the play was initially performed by the city of Vienna around 1784. It was soon blocked due to its content which was considered offensive to nobles and royal family, however Lorenzo da Ponte managed to receive permission from the government to set the opera as opera. Mozart was the one who chose this play as his subject, and then brought the play into da Ponte. Da Ponte, in turn transformed it into the stunning libretto we have today, within six weeks. His most significant change, intended to placate the censors was to replace Figaro's famous climactic rant against inheritable nobility by an equally arousing duet against wifeless wives. Contrary to widespread reports that this libretto actually was accepted by the Emperor prior to the time Mozart made the note. The first performance was held on September 9 and the response of the public was so favorable that they were forced to repeat almost every piece. The issue became so serious that the Emperor issued a decree saying that for the foreseeable future, solos will not be repeated. He also put up a notice to this in the Burgtheater.

The article of the Wiener Realzeitung was extravagant in its praise.
"Mozart's musical compositions are generally loved by aficionados already at the first performance, even if I exclude only those who's self-esteem and pride do not permit them to see merit in any work that is not written by themselves. The general public ... didn't actually know until the very first day of the concert where it stood. They heard many a bravo from uninitiated connoisseurs. However, rude louts from the top of the story sounded their hired lungs to the max with every ounce of force to deafen the audience and singers alike by slapping their St! and Pst. As a result the audience was divided by the conclusion of the performance. (This is in reference at the paid claques which attempted to

disrupt the performance. It is unclear who paid for them, however. The composer was not aware of them. Other than that it is also true that the premiere performance was not the finest, due to the difficulty of the composition. However, now, after a number of performances, one could be falling in line with the cabal or insanity of the music if one were to claim that Mozart's music is not an art masterpiece. It is brimming with beauty and an abundance of ideasthat can only be derived by the power of inborn genius."

The orchestra that plays The Marriage of Figaro is remarkable for its size for the period it was composed to two flutes, two Oboes two bassoons, two clarinets with two horns, two trumpets, timpani and strings. The Requitatives are played with the keyboard, typically either a harpsichord or a fortepiano and the bassline is played by an "cello. It's approximately three hours long, which is quite an amount longer than the operas from the time typically last.

While The Marriage of Figaro seems to have been a bit successful in Vienna however, the premiere took place was held in Prague in the second city in Austria was warmer which was also a routin' success in Prague, which led to a sequel the following year. The outcome from this partnership was Don Giovanni, which was premiering in Prague in 1787, in October to great acclaim, however not as well-received and less success in (again) Vienna in 1788.

Incredibly, when you consider the question in Don Giovanni (many people believe that the Commendatore is a reference to the character Leopold had in Mozart's life) Mozart's father passed away on the 28th of May, 1787.

Mozart was named "chamber composer" to the Emperor Joseph II in December 1787 after the death the composer Gluck who been in this position for a while. It was a temporary appointmentthat paid 800 florins a year and was a requirement for Mozart only to write choreographies to be performed at the annual ball at the Redoutensaal. The income, while not as high as it was proved to be vital to Mozart when the economic downturn hit. According to court documents the purpose of this appointment was in order to make sure that Mozart didn't leave Vienna to pursue greater and more lucrative jobs.

Also in 1787 the young Ludwig van Beethoven spent several weeks in Vienna in search of a class with Mozart.

While no evidence exists to prove that Mozart and Beethoven ever had a conversation The two composers definitely were aware of one another's existence. It's probable for the reason that Beethoven would have wanted to meet Mozart particularly as he was a student with Haydn and wasn't happy.

Don Giovanni

or il dissoluto punito
("The libertine punished") is the title of a two-act musical that features an Italian libretto written by Lorenzo Da Ponte. The story is based on the mythology that tell of Don Juan, a fictional seducer and libertine. It is also based on the famed Venetian love and adventurer Giovanni Casanova who was a close friend and associate with Lorenzo da Ponte when he resided in Venice.

It was the Prague Italian opera premiered it at the National Theater (of Bohemia) that is now the Estates Theatre on 29 October 1787. Da Ponte's libretto is advertised as a dramma-giocoso, the most common title of the time that refers to the combination of comic and serious actions. Mozart however, incorporated the work into his catalogue by virtue of his status as an opera buff. While it is sometimes categorized as comic, the work blends comedy, melodrama, as well as supernatural elements.

It was originally planned to premiere in Prague to benefit from the success in The Marriage of Figaro in the city and also to commemorate the visit of The Duchess Maria Theresa of Austria, the daughter of Emperor Joseph II, and her husband on the 14th of October 1787. The opera was not completed on time, and The Marriage of Figaro was substituted and the premiere occurred a month after. The opera was finished on the 28th or 29th of the month of October. The overture, which is among the most famous in all opera, was completed on the day prior to the premiere or the very date of performance.

The score is for 2 flutes and two Oboes two clarinets and two bassoons as being two trumpets, two horns and three trombones (including alto, tenor, and bass) as well as timpani, basso continuo to accompany the recitatives and strings. The composer also incorporated extra musical effects for example, during the ballroom scene towards the close of Act I two onstage ensembles perform dance music in sync together with orchestra. Each group plays in their own measure (a 3/4 minuet and a 2/4 counterdanse and a quick three-quarter peasant style) and is accompanied by the dance of the principal characters. This feat of genius is among the most remarkable feats in every piece of music, yet it is so simple and well-crafted that it doesn't immediately make an impact on the listener. Its details rather, it's an eloquent statement of the roles of the characters within the opera and their role in the social context that is the stage. Don Giovanni is a nobleman (well it's an impudent nobleman since in the very first scene in which we meet him, he's fleeing from an violence against Donna Anna) and so He dances in the elegant and aristocratic minuet while Zerlina is the peasant girl. She dances the gorgeous yet rustic counterdanse. And her lover, Masetto performs the traditional 3/8 dance of the peasants.

Another masterpiece of music is the serenade that he sings, with the accompaniment of the guitar, with pizzicato strings to accompany. In the following, two performances in The Commendatore ("Di riders finirai in the pria dell'aurora" and "Ribaldo audace, lascia morti the pace") are performed by clarinets, oboes, bassoons and trombones (with basses and 'cellos) which create chilling effects.

The production premiered on October 29 1787, in Prague with the full title Il dissoluto puito ossia Il Don Giovanni - Dramma giocoso in due atti (The Dissolute Punished, which is also Don Giovanni, a comic dramatic play in 2 acts). The production was extremely well-received, with the crowd singing and applauding. It became clear to Mozart that even though there was a lot of intrigue stifling him in Vienna Mozart was loved by the people of Prague. The article of Prager Oberpostamtzeitung read, Prager Oberpostamtzeitung read,

"Connoisseurs and musicians have said that Prague has not heard of anything like this,"
And, to the contrary:
"the the ... can be extremely challenging to stage."
Lorenzo da Ponte was not present at the beginning, as a result, Mozart who conducted from his keyboard, took all the praises.

The production was staged in Vienna it was the final scene of the play, in which the remaining cast members are singing about the way they miss Don Giovanni after he is being dragged to Hell in the hands of the Commendatore who tries to drag him into hell, needed been cut. The moralistic nature of Viennese audience was not as the enjoyment of Don Giovanni's antics that Prague audience enjoyed.

The opera premiered at Vienna on May 7 1788. Mozart composed two new arias, Don Ottavio's song "Dalla sua pace" ("From his peace" KV 540a), composed on the 24th of April for the Tenor Francesco Morella), and Donna Elvira's aria "In the midst of a calamity ... My tradi quello samma ingrata" ("What exaggerations ... He betrayed me , that unregenerate soul" KV 540c composed on the 30th of April to the soprano Caterina Cavalieri) and the duet of Leporello as well as Zerlina "Per Queste Tue Manine" ("For this little hands" KV 540b, composed on the 28th of April). Mozart also made some changes during the Finale to reduce the length, especially the part in which Donna Anna and Ottavio, Donna Elvira, Zerlina, Masetto and Leporello made public their ideas for the coming year ("Or che to all, or mio tesoro" "Now all, my treasure"). is all my treasure"). To connect "Ah sure, certo and l'ombra that I met" ("It must be the ghost that she saw") with "the "moral" in the tale "Questo and the end of Chi Fassione" ("This will be the finality that is awaiting wicked people"), Mozart composed the opera in a different form "Resti dunque quel birbon a la Proserpina and Pluton!" ("So, the wretch will remain down there along with Proserpina or Pluto !"). The cuts are rarely seen in theaters today.

After Don Giovanni

A

For Don Giovanni, despite the massive success of the production, Mozart met one setback every day in his career. The inability of him to get an excellent job in the Imperial Court was partly responsible for his being becoming less sought-after as composer. For instance, one of his performances in 1790 was cancelled because he was unable to not get enough subscriptions. The last three symphonies (39 39, 40 and 41) that are today thought of as his finest compositions for symphonic music were composed for the 1788 concert that is not believed to have been performed.

The summer 1788 was a difficult period for Mozart. He was not only grieving the death of his father as well as the loss of his daughter Theresia and his second daughter Constanze, but he was in deep debt due to the extravagant spending of Mozart and Constanze. Mozart was required by his friend Michael Puchberg, to beg for the loan. Puchberg helped him however Mozart was in dire circumstances and did not regain the financial stability he had enjoyed in his early years.

"Symphony #40" in G minor

M

ozart composed his final three symphonies within a time of seven weeks during his summer in 1788. The third, Symphony in G Minor No. 40, is often known as"the "Great" G minor symphony to differentiate this from "Little" G minor symphony No. 25. They are the only minor-key Symphony that Mozart composed and possibly with the exception of an earlier, but recently discovered A minor symphony, which is known today in the form of the Odense Symphony. This is possibly the most well-known work written by Mozart within the symphonic category However, it is the movement that's more known (the second one is mostly ignored) and is followed by the last movement, which is so thrilling that it literally pops out of the pages. The third movement, also known as the trio and the minuet are quite different from what Mozart typically composes that they're equally remarkable however, the second movement is mostly forgotten.

The Austrian Empire was in war with Turkey which caused people to imagine things that were not music. Personally Mozart's six-month-old daughter Theresia was just killed which threw the family and Mozart in deep sorrow.

Mozart was a crafter who wrote his works on the basis of a commission. He did not receive a commission on these works but they're massive and meticulously crafted (actually it is quite full of small mistakes however, the music is superb) and huge works.

It is possible that he was trying to create an archive of work which he could then use for concerts that were subscription-based. The issue with this theory is that he does not seem to have played the works. It is possible that his old pal Antonio Salieri may have performed at least this symphony during the 1789 subscription concert. There is a possibility that Mozart wanted to be invited to England like Haydn was. He had impressed people and even aristocrats when in England as a kid. Haydn was invited by Salomon to travel to London as the financial (and increasingly also, the creative) capital in Europe and Mozart certainly had a similar idea in his mind. He could have composed this symphony with the two other (39 as well as 41) in order to perform them upon his return to England. Of course, he didn't not live long enough to see it take place, even though G minor was the most popular key. G minor was one that the legendary English composer Johann Christian Bach, with whom Mozart had studied in London was a fan of. His piece is highly complex and complex in its contrapuntal form, (one might say "artificial" in the traditional meaning of the word) and evidently a mathematical minuet rather than a danceable, authentic one. Actually, given the context of the piece it is among the most tragic and sad minuets ever composed. It's amazing how it builds develops to a stunning anti-contrapuntal climax.

It is possible that he - which is not the most likely, but most appealing of options just have felt forced to communicate with his. The fortunes of Mozart had plummeted to the point that Mozart was forced to relocate in the suburbs surrounding Vienna due to his financial troubles, and losing his child the recession in his economy due to the war and his own demise as a "popularity," may have led him into a state of depression as well. The G minor symphony, particular, is sad.

G minor isn't an instrument that Mozart preferred. The most convincing evidence to support it is in the formal aspects of the piece itself - all four of them are unusually - in sonata-allegro forms. The first one is naturally, but the final movement has also been a sonata as is the second tragic movement.

The first movement begins with an accompaniment and soon introduces the primary theme, the principal quasi-baroque motif, dotted with the descending secondary "sighing" motif. The second theme is more sad, and melodic however, it does get out of a mood quite quickly. First subject talked around in the beginning section. The development section is written chromatic and enharmonic chromatic, that begins with the first-group content that is in F minor. When listening to the development section it is easy to remember Mozart's fondness for Bach and his intricate contrapuntal nuances that he learned from London Bach (Johann Christian) and that was certain to be well-known in London. It's like a sincere tribute to his beloved long-dead composer.

It is important to note that the Andante (second move) is not composed in the typical manner that second-movements are written in. It is not a long aria-like tune. It's very tense. Take a listen to for the initial 35 second and you'll feel like an artist working on an idea, not simply stating one. It appears to be discussing the melody. It is interesting to note that the two topics are related - similar to sonata form. Actually, this piece is also a sonata.

The trio and the minuet are so radically opposite that they close to defying the title. The gradual development of the minuet is quite dramatic in the

Mannheim Rocket sort of way. In contrast to the trio that is quiet and beautiful, battling the wind in a peaceful way, it is designed specifically for English audience members of the late 18th century.

The final, the third sonata of this work, is a rocket. It smacks you in a completely un-Classical style. Although the opening is, it can't be as intense as the development section which starts with a bang that's designed to confuse any tone-conscious listener. He spits out diminished chords in a flurry of rage. Then, he chucks us all-in to a four-part contrapuntal that is a work of the music. The utterly breathless nature of this piece will be a huge excitement for the conductor. The bizarre writing for the clarinet (an idea that was conceived as an afterthought to Mozart and cited as proof that he could have performed if you were to write an entire part for clarinets) is a truly original idea.

It is odd that Mozart doesn't have a timpani, and no trumpet in his most explosive of his works. This supports the idea that he was a member of a specific orchestra (maybe one that was an English one, or perhaps it was a reference to the Mannheim one, which consisted of mainly strings, but with a few traces of brass and wind instruments).

The result we're left with is an evocative piece that is incredibly moving and this is just one of two Symphonies Mozart composed in G minor, or, in fact in any major key. It is a work that has numerous aspects of Mozart's mind in its selection of groupings for instruments and its formal structure as well as its key, its quasi-baroque materials, as well as its treatment of contrapuntals. It's a masterpiece that is highly praised 10 years too to be completed.

While he was writing the work, Mozart was troubled by an absence of commissions and also by the passing of his infant daughter Theresia. A letter addressed to lodge brother outlines "dark thoughts I need to expel by force" and, it seems, those thoughts hindered the ability of Mozart to compose. In this summer, Mozart completed very few compositions. The only major work he completed were three symphonies composed in just seven weeks. It would also be his last works of his career.

XI

MOZART'S THE END OF MOZART'S FINAL

<>

Wolfgang Amadeus Mozart

The year 1789 was the time he travelled to Dresden and performed using the organ Bach had played at the Thomaskirche which he later took to Berlin. He was granted a commission to write an opera by the Emperor Joseph II, and once was able to choose Lorenzo da Ponte to write the libretto. Even though Cosi fan tutte was a magnificent work, full of comedy and musical ingenuity it was only performed five times after the Emperor passed away at the end of February in 1790. A time of mourning was in place, putting the performance in limbo, and cost Mozart an enormous amount.

Conclusion

Mozart's life was plagued by illness and financial hardship However, despite these issues, he composed some of the most famous music that the world has ever heard.

In his 35 years on Earth He composed more than 600 compositions, which included 22 operas, 41 symphonies along with 27 piano concertos. The number of compositions would have been higher should he not passed away at an early age.

He was an extremely talented musician, and his amazing music was able to flow effortlessly from him, continues to be admirated and admired by fans from all over the world.

www.ingramcontent.com/pod-product-compliance
Lightning Source LLC
Chambersburg PA
CBHW050406120526
44590CB00015B/1854